Smart Skills: Mastering the Numbers

Anne Hawkins started her career as an apprentice in a multinational engineering group where she qualified as an accountant. She then held senior positions in a range of sectors before starting her own training business. She has developed an enviable reputation for explaining financial matters in simple terms. Passionate about her subject and the leverage to be gained by ensuring that everyone in the organisation understands the financial implications of the choices they are making, Anne has also written a number of successful business books, including *Lean Means Beans* (2003) and *100 Great Cost-Cutting Ideas* (2010). She is the co-writer of the *Balance Sheet Pocketbook* (2010).

Other books in the Smart Skills series

Meetings
Persuasion
Negotiation
Presentations
Working With Others

www.smartskillsbooks.com

Smart Skills: Mastering the Numbers

Anne Hawkins

RUPA

Copyright © Anne Hawkins 2011

First published in India in 2012 by
Rupa Publications India Pvt. Ltd.
7/16, Ansari Road, Daryaganj
New Delhi 110 002

Sales Centres:
Allahabad Bengaluru Chennai
Hyderabad Jaipur Kathmandu
Kolkata Mumbai

First published in 2011 by Legend Business, London, UK.

This edition published by arrangement
with the original publisher.

All rights reserved.
No part of this publication may be reproduced, stored in
a retrieval system, or transmitted, in any form or by any
means, electronic, mechanical, photocopying, recording or
otherwise, without the prior permission of the publishers.

10 9 8 7 6 5 4 3 2 1

Anne Hawkins asserts the moral right to be
identified as the author of this work.

This edition is for sale in India only.

CONTENTS

Foreword	7
Introduction	9
1. The Overview	11
2. The Balance Sheet	19
3. The Profit and Loss Account	34
4. The Cash Flow Statement	48
5. Financial Ratios and other Measures of Performance	62
6. Budgeting	75
7. Costing	81
8. Capital Expenditure Appraisal (CAPEX)	99
Dictionary of Accounting Jargon	114
Appendices	119

Foreword

Myriads of management handbooks in print purport to provide guidance on the key skills for success and business training manuals also abound. Generally, they suffer from one or both of two defects.

Sometimes, the scope of the book is too broad. Attempting to provide comprehensive advice on all the basic business activities, there is no clear message. Nobody can gain proficiency in every field of marketing and sales, administration, purchasing, book-keeping and financial management in a short period of time, although those who start their own businesses do need to acquire a working knowledge of most. Other titles fail to distinguish between technical capability and personal skills.

There are similar problems with books offering comprehensive advice on the "numbers" management of business which are the essential skills that entrepreneurs and managers of any size of business, as well as management consultants, need to acquire in order to be successful. Although the subject matter is more specialised, there is a difficult balance to be achieved between over-simplification and burdening readers with too much technical accounting detail. In *Mastering the Numbers* Anne Hawkins has trod the tightrope safely; her book is written with great clarity and provides a mixture of good common sense and detail of the accounting and financial topics with which readers will want to be fully conversant.

Like the other subjects in the Smart Skills series all readers can focus to their advantage as mastery of the skills will surely enhance both job satisfaction and their careers.

Jonathan Reuvid

Introduction

This is not a book for accountants.

Neither is it a book for those wanting to learn about the technicalities of book-keeping or the intricacies of published financial accounts.

It is however the book you've been looking for if any of the following strike a chord:

- you're an entrepreneur with a great business idea but are not sure how to explain your plans to the bank or potential investors; or
- you've been promoted up through an organisation to a point at which it's embarrassing to admit you don't understand the financials; or
- you're fed up with going to ask the accountant a question and coming away more confused than you were to begin with; or
- you'd like to understand the meaning of accounting jargon in simple, straight-forward, commonsense terms.

'The numbers' are not created by accountants. They are the culmination of the myriad of choices made by the decision-makers in the business. If you want to master the numbers you'll need to understand how the numbers are compiled, what they are telling you and then use that knowledge to bring them under your control.

This is what this book will help you do.

Note: words in *italics* are included in the Dictionary of Accounting Jargon on p.114.

1. THE OVERVIEW

The 'money-go-round'

Businesses use money to make money.

- Money is brought into the business;
- to buy the things the business needs;
- to create products or services to sell to customers;
- on which the business can earn a profit;
- so there is additional money available to invest;
- so the business can buy more of the things it needs;
- so it can make more products or deliver more services to customers;
- so it can make even more profit;
- so that there is yet more money available to invest …

It's a profit-generating 'money-go-round'.

Before looking at 'the numbers' it's helpful to look at the above process in a little more detail starting with the different types of long-term finance the business might use.

WHERE DO BUSINESSES GET THEIR MONEY FROM?
Every business has to have some form of long-term finance to provide them with the capital to buy the things they need. This finance usually consists of a combination of Share Capital, Loans and Retained Profits.

| Share Capital | Loans | Retained Profit |

Share Capital
The shareholders own the business but will appoint a board of directors to run the business on their behalf. They buy shares in the hope of earning an income on their investment (dividends) and growth in the value of their investment as a result of increasing share prices. As owners, they are the risk-takers and therefore last in the 'pecking order' when it comes to getting a share of the profits. [For more on the implications to the business of having shareholders to satisfy see Appendix 1, Share Capital.]

Loans
When money is borrowed, a contract is signed committing the business to pay interest and repay the capital as and when it falls due. To ensure contractual obligations are met, the lender will look for some form of security or collateral.

If the business is unable to use the borrowed money profitably to generate the profits and cash to make the agreed payments the bank may move in, sell off some of the business assets to recover the debt and there may be no business left. Hence borrowing money brings financial risk into the business so this risk needs to be managed. [For more information on the financial implications of taking on loans see Appendix 2, Loans.]

Retained Profit
If the business can make sufficient profit to cover all their costs, there will be money left over for reinvestment. This is the most cost-effective way to grow the business as it results in additional funding being made available without having to attract additional share capital (with resulting pressures from shareholders for higher dividends and more growth) or having to increase the financial risk and interest costs to the business by taking on more loans. So profit is not a dirty word. Far from it. The more long-term finance that can be generated internally the better.

The total amount of long-term finance is known as Net Capital Employed.

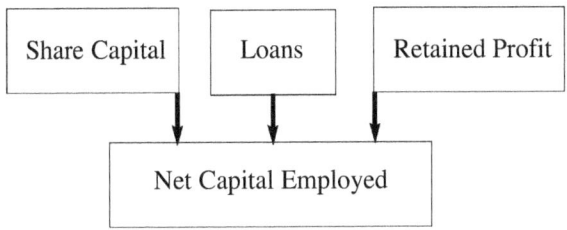

The relative proportions supplied by shareholders as opposed to lenders is referred to as *gearing* and will influence the business' financial risk.

WHAT DO THEY USE THE MONEY FOR?

The management team will determine the way in which the funds raised are invested. These decisions will reflect the design of the products or services and the way the business is being run. Some of the items purchased, for example equipment, will be 'one-off' items intended to be of use to the business over a number of years (i.e. *Fixed Assets*), whereas others such as materials and labour will be of a 'repeat purchase' nature (i.e. *Working Capital*).

The total amount invested in Fixed Assets and Working Capital is known as Net Assets Employed.

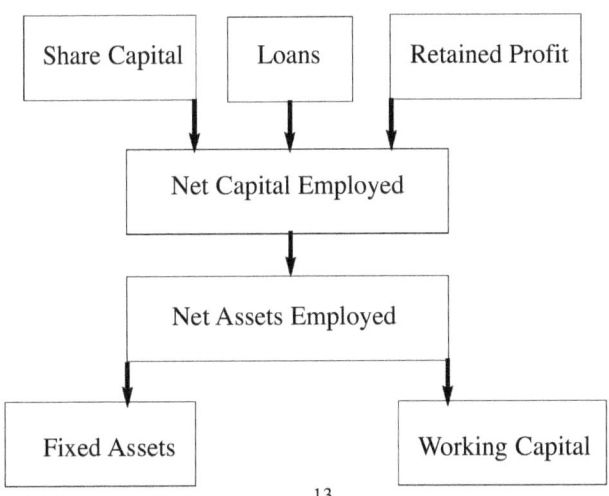

Fixed Assets (also known as Non-current Assets)

The selection of these items is a strategic decision as it sets out the way the business intends to make products or deliver services for potentially many years into the future. As a result, the authorisation process for such *capital expenditure* is challenging (see Chapter 8, Capital Investment Appraisal).

Fixed assets are purchased with the intention of keeping them and using them over a number of years to provide the business with a chosen capability for making and delivering products or services. Therefore it makes sense that rather than putting the total cost of these items into the calculation of profit in the year of purchase, the cost is 'spread' over the useful life to the business to produce an annual charge against profit. This charge is known as *depreciation* or *amortisation*. [For more information on the importance of choosing the right capability and the accounting treatment for these Fixed Assets, see Appendix 3.]

Working Capital

Revenue expenditure provides the business with the materials, labour, bought-in services and expenses it needs to produce its products or deliver its services. Although the aim is to 'pull' these costs through the business as quickly as possible by turning them into products or services customers pay for, at any point in time some will be 'trapped' in the *Working Capital Cycle*.

This cycle follows the flow of cash through the business and back into cash again.

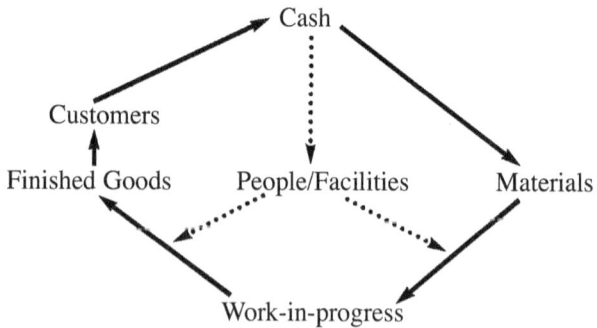

Cash is used to buy materials and pay for the cost of converting them into the products or services the market wants. Goods or services are then sold and cash comes back into the business.

The cycle is usually more complex as materials may be purchased on credit (delaying the outflow of cash) and customers may have negotiated credit with the business (delaying the inflow of cash).

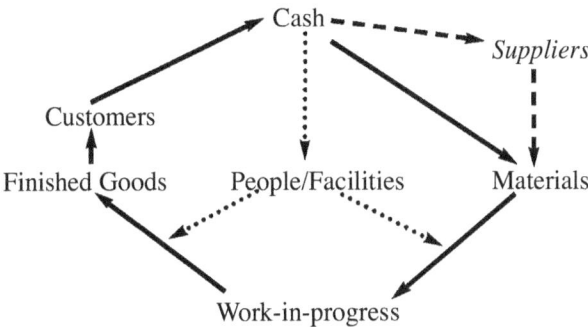

The amount of money tied up in the cycle at any point in time is therefore determined by taking the amount of cash being held; plus the value of inventory (materials plus work-in-progress plus finished goods); plus the value of goods or services that have been delivered to customers but not yet paid for; less the amount of credit from suppliers (i.e. the invoice value of materials that have been received and are therefore in inventory but for which the business has not yet paid.)

A detailed explanation of the cycle and Working Capital terminology is given in Appendix 4, Working Capital.

ARE THEY MAKING MONEY?

The fixed assets and working capital are then put to use to make products or services that can be sold. The total value of sales, or invoices raised in a period, may be referred to as *turnover* or *revenue*.

The next step is to compare the value of sales with the costs incurred in making those products or delivering those services to determine whether the business has made a profit. Included in these costs is not just the cost of materials, labour, expenses etc. but also depreciation, that 'fair and reasonable allocation' of the amount of money invested in providing the business with its capability, as explained above. If the business has got it right, the market will reward it for choosing to organise itself appropriately with selling prices exceeding costs. [Different approaches to calculating product or service costs are explained in Chapter 7 , Costing.]

The profit figure at this stage is often referred to as Operating Profit as the financing costs have yet to come.

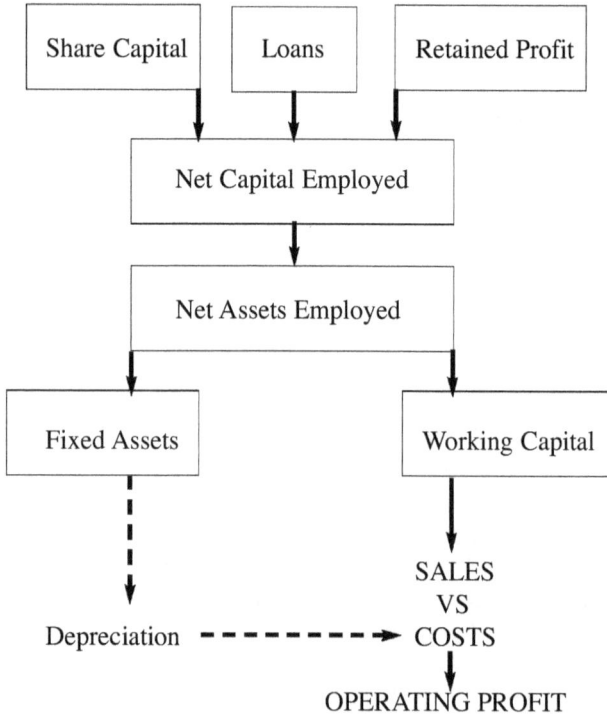

Deducted from the Operating Profit are firstly the costs of interest payments on the loans and then the tax that has to be paid on any profits. The profit measure at this stage is referred to as Earnings and belongs to the shareholders. Some of this they will want to take as dividends, with the rest available to reinvest back into the business as Retained Profit.

Smart Skills: Mastering the Numbers

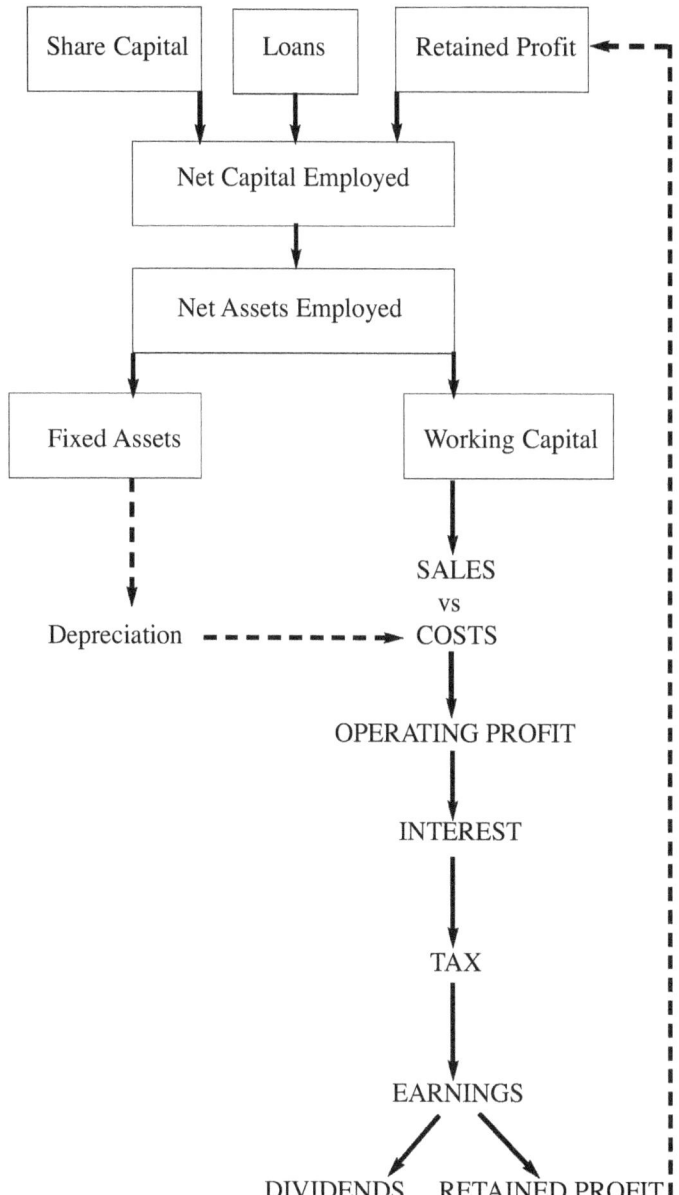

So now you have a more detailed version of the 'money-go-round'.

Businesses raise capital to invest in providing themselves with both the capability (Fixed Assets) and materials, labour and other costs (Working Capital) to make products or provide services.

They work this investment to make products or organise services which they can sell to customers at a profit.

Sufficient profit to cover all their business and financial costs and have something left over to reinvest back into the business to, for example, buy a new machine.

So that next year they can make and sell more products or services so that they can make more profit so that they have even more left over to reinvest back into the business ...

This is a powerful 'money-making machine' and needs mastering.

- The Balance Sheet reports on 'the numbers' in the first part of the model by setting out where the business has got its finance from (Net Capital Employed) and how that money is currently invested (Net Assets Employed).
- The Profit & Loss Account covers the second section, setting out how well the management team have used that investment to generate sales and profit.

[*A word of warning:* The focus so far has been on making a profit – i.e. selling products for more than they cost. However, businesses do not go into receivership because they make a loss but because they run out of cash. As profit and cash flow are not the same thing (and can even move in opposite directions), mastering the profit numbers is not enough.

If you're going to run your business in such a way that you don't just make a profit but you also generate cash you'll also need to master the'levers' to be found in the Cash Flow Statement (see p.53).]

2. THE BALANCE SHEET

or Statement of Financial Position

INTRODUCTION
The Balance Sheet does not tell you what the business is worth. It is a statement at a point in time of where the money came from to finance the business and where that money is currently tied up and reports on the first part of the 'money-making machine' modelled in the previous chapter. (See diagram on p.13.)

The Balance Sheet is called a Balance Sheet because it balances. You can't have money that's come in (from shareholders, lenders or through retaining profits) but then disappears, neither can you have spent money you never had.

READING THE BALANCE SHEET
All balance sheets (or Statements of Financial Position) are snapshots at a point in time showing where the money came from and where it is currently invested.

One of the challenges to those trying to read and interpret them is that not all statements are presented in the same format. This can, at first sight, be confusing. But the 'building blocks' remain the same. Therefore this section will focus on the key items that go into the Balance Sheet and how they are valued rather than deliberating too much on matters of presentation.

Here is a 'skeleton' Balance Sheet in a commonly used format:

	£
Fixed Assets	290,000
Working Capital	<u>210,000</u>
<u>Net Assets Employed</u>	£500,000
	£
Share Capital	48,000
Retained Profits	252,000
Loans	<u>200,000</u>
<u>Net Capital Employed</u>	£500,000

The first thing to notice is that the two halves have been reversed from the extract of the model shown on p.13. 'Where the money came from' is now on the bottom and 'Where the money is now' is on the top.

The Balance Sheet must balance. If it doesn't, someone has made a clerical error. Heard accountants talk about "double-entry book-keeping"? That's because for every financial transaction there will always be two entries in the accountant's books:

Either matching increases to both the top and bottom halves:
e.g. selling additional shares

　　　　Share Capital　↑　Cash (included in Working Capital) ↑

or matching decreases to both the top and bottom halves:
e.g. repaying a loan

　　　　Loans　↓　Cash　　　　　　　　　　　　　　↓

or equal and opposite entries within the same halves;
e.g. buying new equipment

　　　　Fixed Assets　↑　Cash　　　　　　　　　　　↓

Here's that Balance Sheet in a little more detail.

	£	£
Fixed Assets:		
Land and buildings	165,000	
Equipment	125,000	
		290,000
Current Assets:		
Inventory	100,000	
Receivables	180,000	
Cash	5,000	
	285,000	
Current Liabilities:		
Payables	75,000	
Working Capital		210,000
Net Assets Employed		£500,000
Share Capital	48,000	
Retained Profits	252,000	
Net Worth		300,000
Loans		200,000
Net Capital Employed		£500,000

Start with the totals.

A Balance Sheet will have two balancing equal entries so start by identifying those. In this case there is £500,000 of Net Assets Employed ('Where the money is now') and £500,000 of Net Capital Employed ('Where the money came from to buy those things').

Now move into the analysis of these figures starting with the totals in the right-hand column.

The top half of the statement shows where the money is currently invested and here the total of £500,000 comprises £290,000 Fixed

Assets and £210,000 Working Capital.

The £290,000 Fixed Assets comprises £165,000 Land and Buildings and £125,000 Equipment.

Working Capital is the net of Current Assets and Current Liabilities (see Appendix 4, Working Capital). In this case £210,000 Working Capital is the net result of £285,000 Current Assets minus £75,000 Current Liabilities.

The Current Assets total of £285,000 comprises £100,000 Inventory (or Stock) £180,000 Receivables (or Debtors) and £5,000 Cash.

As for the Current Liabilities, here there is just one figure of £75,000 for Payables (or Creditors).

Turning to the bottom half of this Balance Sheet format, the statement shows where the money came from to buy the things in the top half. It is important to understand that there is no money to be 'found' in the items shown in this part of the statement – the statement just sets out where the money originally came from.

You can't walk around the business and find the share capital. There's a register of shareholders' names and the number of shares they own but no actual money.

Neither can you find the loans. There are statements from lenders giving values for the loans outstanding but no bundle of £ notes.

Nor can you find the retained profits. You can check back through the Profit and Loss Account over the years to see how much has been reinvested over the life of the business but you're not going to find a pot of money marked "profit", because that money has already been and gone. Look at the top half of the statement again. The profits are up there in the form of new equipment, inventory… and some may (but not necessarily – see p.48) be there as cash.

A warning note: The figure in the Balance Sheet for Retained Profit is cumulative over the life of the business to date. If the business has been successful this value could be very large. Confusingly, this sum of cumulative retained profit is often referred to as Reserves.

[To be pedantic, Reserves is actually a collective term that covers a number of different items but by far the most important to you is that of cumulative retained profits.]

To the layman this use of the word Reserves might imply that there is a large sum of money put by for emergencies.

Not the case at all. There is no cash in Reserves.

The rationale, accountants would argue, behind the use of the word is that, as shown in the diagram on p.17, Retained Profits represent the profits left over for shareholders that, rather than being taken out as dividends, have been 'reserved' for reinvestment back within the business.

So you need to be careful that this unfortunate choice of jargon doesn't result in your having a very false impression of a business' financial security.

Looking back at the statement it can be seen that £48,000 Share Capital and £252,000 Retained Profits are added together to give a sub-total called Net Worth (also known as Shareholders' Funds) of £300,000.

The reason for doing this is to differentiate between the finance that has come from shareholders (either by buying shares or allowing their profits to be reinvested) and the amount that has come from loans.

Once the Loans of £200,000 are added to Net Worth the total, Net Capital Employed, explains where the capital came from to buy those Fixed Assets and Working Capital shown on the top half of the statement.

[If you're still uneasy about the different formats the Balance Sheet can be presented in, take a look at Appendix 5 to see that whilst the layout and sub-totals and terminology may change, 'the numbers' remain the same.]

INTERPRETING THE NUMBERS

"A snapshot at a point in time" ... and therein lies one of the limitations of the Balance Sheet. Those running the business know when the snapshot is to be taken (sometimes monthly, maybe quarterly and certainly twice a year for the shareholders) and although the camera never lies – and the auditors come in to check that's the case – neither does it necessarily give a realistic portrayal of what the business looks like on a 'typical' day. Just as you prepare for a photograph (by looking as professional as you can for a business photograph, or maybe as relaxed as possible for that 'happy family' shot) so too does the business prepare for the event by making itself look as attractive as possible.

The phrase "Get it out the door!" can be heard reverberating throughout the business as everyone scrambles to get the sales (and hence the profits) into the accounts. Inventory levels are reduced, payments are chased up from customers and payments to suppliers are strung out as long as possible. Be aware of these 'window-dressing' tactics when interpreting the numbers.

Before going any further it is important to emphasise again that the Balance Sheet does not give you the 'value' of the business.

What is something worth? Your house, your car?
It's worth what someone would pay to buy it.

It's just the same with a business. If you own the shares you own the business. Therefore a business is 'worth' the number of shares multiplied by the market price for the shares as that is the price you would have to pay to buy it (see Appendix 1, Share Capital).

Just as with any statistical analysis, before using 'the numbers' to interpret what is happening in the business, you need to understand the basis on which they're compiled. In this case it's important to know how the assets and liabilities are valued.

Valuation of Net Assets Employed
Valuation of Fixed Assets
[For an in-depth explanation of the terminology and accounting treatment of Fixed Assets see Appendix 3.]

In the example on the next page, a business buys a piece of equipment for £50,000 intending to use it in the business for 5 years resulting in a *depreciation* charge of £10,000 p.a. to be made against profit. The valuation of the equipment on the Balance Sheet (where it is shown at NBV – see below) falls over time as a result of the depreciation charge as follows:

| | **Year 1** | **Year 2** | **Year 3** | **Year 4** | **Year 5** |
	£	£	£	£	£
Cost	50,000	50,000	50,000	50,000	50,000
Cumulative Depreciation	10,000	20,000	30,000	40,000	50,000
NBV	40,000	30,000	20,000	10,000	0

This is important. Look at how the NBV (Net Book Value) is just the result of taking the cost of the equipment less the cumulative depreciation charge to date. It is effectively the 'stock' of fixed asset cost that has yet to be charged against profit. This will not be the same as the saleable value of the asset and therefore should not be viewed as the amount of money the business could realise if they sold it off.

What if the equipment referred to in the example above was a purpose-built press to make a product that nobody else in the world produces in that way? The equipment cost £50,000 and is being depreciated over 5 years so it would be valued in the books at the end of the first year at £40,000. Yet the resale value is probably zero – and indeed the business may have to pay someone to take it away!

It can be difficult to predict useful life accurately. If the equipment above were to be depreciated over 10 years rather than 5, the annual charge would be £5,000 rather than £10,000. As depreciation is a cost that is charged against profit, the number of years chosen will not just affect the Balance Sheet value but also how much profit is declared. The aim is to make the predicted useful life realistic so that the profit figure will provide a fair assessment of whether customers are willing to pay a price that rewards the business not just for the costs incurred for materials, people etc. but also for the investment made in providing the capability to make and deliver those products or services.

If useful life is overestimated then there will be an asset left on your books that is no longer of any use and when that residual cost is written off it will reduce profits. On the other hand, if the useful life is underestimated, then products or services will be over-costed in the early years and under-costed in later years resulting in a distorted picture of where you are making money and therefore the potential for poor decisions concerning your product or service portfolio.

Valuation of Working Capital

[For an in-depth explanation of the investment in Working Capital and the Working Capital cycle see Appendix 4.]

One of the fundamental accounting principles is that of prudency or conservatism. (This is what is responsible for giving accountants the rather unattractive image of being negative, pessimistic, miserable individuals who are always on the look-out for bad news.)

Charged with producing statements to guide others on the financial position of the business, they are required, where there is some uncertainty, to understate rather than overstate how well the business is doing. If there is potentially bad news (e.g. a possible claim against the business) they are required to immediately account for it appropriately – whereas if there is good news (e.g. a large profitable order) they cannot take the benefit until it has actually happened.

Inventory

Here is a clear example of 'prudency' at work. Inventory must be valued at the lower of cost and net realisable value (i.e how much you can sell it for).

So if you are holding inventory that you will be unable to sell for at least what it cost you, you will have to 'write it down' to its saleable value. (Note that this write-off is a cost that will reduce profit.) This means that in many businesses the figure shown on the Balance Sheet is referred to as Net Inventory – i.e. Gross Inventory (the cost of all the inventory you have) less any provisions for scrap, obsolescence etc.

If on the other hand you are holding inventory that you know you will be able to sell at a profit, you must continue to hold it on your Balance Sheet at cost until it is actually sold.

Receivables

This is the amount of money you are waiting to receive for goods or services that have been invoiced to your customers but for which you have not yet been paid.

Once again accountants must be prudent in the value they attribute to this asset by combing through these invoices to identify those where there is uncertainty that the customer will eventually pay. They then create a bad debt provision reducing the value of the receivables asset on the Balance Sheet and matching it by reducing profit.

Cash

The amount of cash you hold – including that in the bank account.

Payables

This is the amount of money you owe other people that has to be paid in the short-term (i.e. within 12 months).

Those amounts you owe your suppliers for buying in the materials and services you then ultimately sell on to the customer are referred to as Trade Creditors. Other creditors may include any bank overdraft and amounts owed (but hopefully not yet due) for tax and dividend payments.

Valuation of Net Capital Employed

Share Capital

Share Capital is valued on the Balance Sheet at its Nominal Value – i.e. at the unit of value given on the share certificate. So if a business has 100,000 shares with a nominal share price of £1, unless additional shares are issued (or shares that are surplus to requirements 'bought back') the share capital will remain on the Balance Sheet at a value of £100,000 regardless of the current market price of the share. [For an explanation of why the ups and downs of the stock market do not have an impact on the Balance Sheet value of the business, see Appendix 1, Share Capital.]

Retained Profit

This is the cumulative figure, over the life of the business to date, of the profits that have been available, after all the costs have been met, to reinvest back within the business. (See Chapter 3, Profit & Loss Account.)

Loans

This represents the total value of long-term loans the business currently has.

***

Balancing the books

Do note that there is no 'balancing entry'. When assets increase or decrease in value there is always an equal and opposite impact on another item on the statement, keeping the Balance Sheet balanced.

Here are some examples of this reflecting the way assets are valued:

- If £10 inventory has gone past its use-by date, under the prudency principle (see above) it has to be written-off. The value of inventory is reduced by £10, obsolescence costs increase by £10 and hence profit falls by £10.
- When fixed assets are depreciated, the assets decrease in value and the charge for depreciation, being a cost of running the business, reduces profit.
- If inventory is purchased for £80 and then sold to a customer on credit for £100, the assets go up by £20 (as £80 inventory is replaced by £100 receivables) and the profit goes up by £20 as shown by the extracts from the Balance Sheet below:

		Step 1 Buy item for £80	Step 2 Sell item for £100
Inventory	–	£80	–
Receivables	–	–	£100
Cash	£80	–	–
Total	**£80**	**£80**	**£100**
Share Capital	£80	£80	£80
Profit	–	–	£20
Total	**£80**	**£80**	**£100**

When the customer pays, the assets just reconfigure with no impact on profit:

Step 3
Customer pays

Inventory	–	–
Receivables	£100	–
Cash	–	£100
Total	**£100**	**£100**
Share Capital	£80	£80
Profit	£20	£20
Total	**£100**	**£100**

Note that the profit is declared when the goods or services are invoiced, not when the customer pays. Perhaps accountants are not being as prudent as they think!

This timing issue is very important when it comes to looking at the difference between profit and cash flow (see p.48)

MASTERING THE BALANCE SHEET INVESTMENT

The Balance Sheet is just one piece of the jigsaw that pictures the financial health of the business. In the absence of some of the other pieces (and importantly an understanding of what the business does), it is hard to judge how well a business is performing.

For example, without a profit figure it is difficult to comment on whether the scale of the investment is appropriate in relation to the profits it has been used to generate. Without a sales figure it is difficult to judge whether the business is holding an appropriate level of stock and successfully managing the amount of credit it allows its customers.

As explained on p.24, the total value shown on the Balance Sheet, the figure on which the statement balances, is not what the business is worth.

So far from wanting the 'biggest' balance sheet you can manage, you actually want as little as possible. Every £1 invested in the business had to come from somewhere (e.g. a shareholder or a bank) and therefore comes at a financial cost so you want to run your business with as little investment as possible whilst keeping your customers happy.

Keep watching the marketplace and aligning your business accordingly. The market may set the price for your products or services but you determine the cost and hence it's up to you whether you make a profit or not. The customer pays a price that rewards suppliers for doing things efficiently and effectively. They do not pay a premium just because, for example, their supplier uses inappropriate equipment or surrounds himself with a load of unnecessary slow-moving inventory.

Your choice of processes (Fixed Assets) and the way you organise making and delivering your products or services (Working Capital) determine how much investment you need. This is the Goldilocks approach: Not too much. Not too little. Just right. Too much investment (over-capitalisation) and your assets work sluggishly so you end up carrying unnecessary financial burdens that your customer will not pay for in his price. Too little investment (under-capitalisation) and you're forever scrabbling around on a financial knife-edge perpetually hitting your overdraft limit.

To master these Balance Sheet numbers you need to keep challenging your investment to find better ways of doing more with less.

Fixed Assets

As you've seen, on the balance sheet, Fixed Assets are valued at cost less the cumulative depreciation charged to date. For an individual item, this sum represents the share of the original cost that has yet to deliver value to the business through providing a capability to make and deliver the company's products or services.

This NBV of the asset isn't what you're really interested in here as this future depreciation charge is a "sunk cost" – i.e. one that you can't do anything about unless you choose to dispose of the asset and accept the resultant write-off of the NBV against profit.

Instead take a look at the Fixed Asset register that lists each individual item the business owns:

- Have you got the right capability?
- Are you using this investment efficiently and effectively?
- Are there items in the register that you no longer need?

Remember that even if unwanted items have a value on the books yet little or no resale value, the 'profit hit' may be worth taking if it means you can free up space and reduce clutter. What could you do with this space? Take on new business? Rationalise the site? Save on other storage costs?

If you want to master the investment in Fixed Assets you also need to make sure that anything new you buy will pull its weight. Take a look at some of the techniques available to help you do this in Chapter 8, Capital Expenditure Appraisal.

Working Capital

Inventory

If inventory is an asset why do you want as little as possible? Firstly, because every £1 invested in inventory had to come from somewhere and therefore has a financial cost attached. Secondly, because it will result in additional running costs as you have to control it, store it, safeguard it and make sure it doesn't deteriorate.

But, more importantly, because inventory represents risk. By exchanging cash for inventory you increase the risk to the business. What happens if the market changes and those items are no longer required to meet customer demands? What if you change your design or the way you deliver your services and that inventory becomes obsolete?

A word of warning. Before you slash the level of inventory you hold, remember that there is only one person who brings cash into your business. Your customer. Therefore you want to hold the minimum amount of inventory you can consistent with being able to make on-time deliveries to keep your customer happy.

A further word of warning. The amount of inventory you are holding is the consequence of the way you have organised the timing and volume of the flow of goods and services through your business. It's relatively easy to cut inventory levels in the short-term by holding back purchase orders for a while but a few months later you'll probably find your inventory levels are back where they started. To take inventory out of the business – and keep it out – you need to make changes to the way you organise that flow.

Receivables

Almost there – but not quite. When you invoice your goods or services to your customers the invoice value goes into your sales figure and you calculate and declare the profit you have made.

But have you achieved any real financial benefit yet? All you have done is move some of your assets into your customer's warehouse. It's your money that's still tied up. Until the customer pays for what you've sold him you have not finished the job! If you can sell for cash that's great. If you can't then look to negotiate the shortest terms you can. Customers don't take credit – you agree it by negotiation. If necessary evaluate the trade-off between price and credit-terms. It may pay you to shave a little off the price to collect the cash that bit faster. If you have long-term contracts then go for stage-payments wherever possible.

And, once you've agreed terms, make sure customers stick to them. Don't give them excuses not to pay. Deliver a quality product or service on time with the correct paperwork – and don't forget to invoice them!

Be professional about the way you manage customer credit. Build relationships not just with the buyers in your customers' businesses but also with those involved in the payment process so that you can 'nurse' your invoices through their system to make sure you get paid on time.

Cash

Much as accountants love cash (see p48) you don't want too much of it. After all, what's the point of raising money to invest in a business just for that investment to sit around as cash? Your investors may as well have just put their money in the bank – and you become a target for takeover as others see the opportunity to put this cash to better use. But neither do you want too little of it as that will result in you lurching from one cash flow crisis to another and hefty overdraft charges as well.

Payables

Working Capital is the net of Current Assets and Current Liabilities. So taking credit from your suppliers means you can finance some of your inventory (and if you're lucky even your receivables) with someone else's money. That's got to be a good thing.

But don't overdo it. Firstly there's probably a trade-off here between price and payment terms so make sure you get it right from your point of view. Secondly make sure you take credit through negotiated terms. Just not paying suppliers tends to backfire as it not only puts you in a poor negotiating position for price reviews and if for any reason supply is constrained but it also causes you wasted time, energy and capacity when they put you on "stop" (i.e. suspend deliveries until you have paid). Your defence against such sanctions? You'll end up having to lay in additional inventory to act as a buffer – which brings in additional cost and risk to the business (see above).

Whilst making sure all those assets are working hard and pulling their weight it's also important to master the way they are being financed. It's time to turn your attention to the section of the Balance Sheet that reports on where the money came from.

Take a look at your *gearing,* the relative proportions of finance supplied by lenders as opposed to shareholders. A business with high gearing has lots of borrowing with relatively little shareholder investment; a business with low gearing has relatively little borrowing with a high proportion of its assets being financed by shareholder money.

Loans represent 'third party cold-blooded contractual' money coming from those who have a right to a return on their investment (interest payments) whether the company has a good year or not. Shareholders on the other hand, because they own the business, are the risk-takers. With no contractual right to a return they are last in the 'pecking order' for a share of the profits. So the higher the gearing in your business the greater the financial risk as even in difficult times interest payments will have to be met or your business risks the lender exercising their rights to seize any collateral they have secured on the loan.

Conversely, if your business has low gearing (and is coping with its existing interest payments easily – see p.40, Interest Cover) it is said to have leverage – the ability to take on additional borrowing. This is a good position to be in as borrowing money is a quick way to bring in additional capital to, for example, seize an opportunity to grow the business either through taking on additional orders or through acquisition.

3. THE PROFIT AND LOSS ACCOUNT

or Income Statement

INTRODUCTION
Whereas the Balance Sheet reports how your business is financed and how you've chosen to invest that money, the Profit and Loss Account tells you how well you've used that investment in Fixed Assets and Working Capital to create profits by making and delivering products or services to your customers. Whilst the Balance Sheet is a snapshot at a point in time, the Profit and Loss Account covers a specific period of time (usually a month, quarter, half-year, financial year or financial year-to-date).

The statement starts at the top with the value of your sales and finishes with the amount of profit left over for the shareholders (usually referred to as Earnings or Profit After Tax). A separate statement then sets out how much of the Earnings has been taken out of the business as dividends and how much has therefore been left over, after all your costs have been met, to reinvest back into the business

The information that goes into the externally published Profit and Loss Account is summarised rather than detailed which, amongst other things, avoids potentially highly sensitive commercial information being made available to competitors. Profit and Loss Accounts produced for internal purposes do not usually cover the full range of costs but focus instead in more detail on the cost of operating the business.

READING THE PROFIT LOSS ACCOUNT
External Format
As with the Balance Sheet, the format and jargon used in the statement

will vary between businesses but the essentials, of starting with sales then step-by-step taking account of the business costs, remains the same.

	£
Sales	1,000,000
Cost of Sales	700,000
Gross Profit	300,000
Distribution costs	85,000
Administration expenses	115,000
Operating Profit	100,000
Interest	20,000
Profit Before Tax	80,000
Tax	16,000
Profit After Tax	64,000

The statement starts with the total value of all the invoiced sales during the period that may also be referred to as turnover or revenue. As you proceed down the statement, you 'take the temperature' by measuring profit at different stages as you take account of more and more of the business costs.

The first costs to be deducted from the sales are the Cost of Sales (COS) – those costs directly associated with making the products or services that have been sold (e.g. labour, materials and running costs). Gross Profit is the result of deducting this Cost of Sales figure from the Sales. Notes to the accounts may provide more detail of the costs that have gone into the value for COS. Amongst these costs are *depreciation* and *amortisation* – the charges that result from the accountant, for the purposes of the Profit and Loss Account, spreading the purchase price of fixed assets (e.g. equipment and buildings) over their useful life to the business rather than putting all the costs into the year of purchase.

After Gross Profit come costs such as distribution (including sales and marketing costs) and administration expenses that are part of the operating costs of running the business, but are not seen as activities that are directly associated with making products or delivering services. The profit level at this stage is known as Operating Profit or Earnings Before Interest and Tax (EBIT).

From Operating Profit, the cost of interest on any borrowed money is deducted arriving at Profit Before Tax (PBT).

Once the tax is deducted you are left with Profit After Tax (PAT) or Earnings, which is the amount of money left over for the shareholders who, as the risk-takers in the business, get whatever's left over after everyone else has had their costs met.

The final step (which will usually be shown in a separate statement) sets out how much of the shareholders' profits (i.e. Earnings) has been paid out to them as dividends and hence how much they have agreed to reinvest back within the business.

Internal format

Take a look again at the summarised nature of the above statement. You couldn't run your business without much more detailed information on how you're performing. Therefore statements published for internal use will go into a great deal more detail and will focus on that part of the statement over which the local management team are deemed to be accountable – usually just as far as Operating Profit.

That's why Operating Profit is commonly referred to as "the bottom line".

As you have seen, it's not in reality the bottom line. There are more deductions to come. However, these deductions (interest, tax and ultimately dividends) are usually considered to be the result of decisions outside the remit of the local management team and therefore not something over which they should be judged.

The 'customer' for the internal statement is not the shareholder or the government but local managers. The format and level of detail into which the internal statement goes should be driven by the needs of managers for information they can use in their decision-making. There is no 'rule book' for how these internal reports must be prepared – just a requirement that they should 'mirror the reality' of the comparison between the price the market has been prepared to pay for the goods or services that have been delivered to them and the cost of the resources the business has consumed in achieving those sales.

Every business is different. No two companies bring in the same materials, then use identical equipment and skills to turn them into identical products or services for identical customers. Therefore each business should have a way of costing its products or services that is 'tailor-made' rather than 'off-the-peg'. There are however some common approaches to the way this is done.

Some businesses start by deducting the variable costs (those that vary with the volume of sales – e.g. materials) from the value of sales to determine what is known as the contribution. The contribution has to cover the fixed costs of the business (those that do not vary with the volume of sales – e.g. rent) with any surplus being profit.

Others might use a traditional overhead absorption costing system where overhead costs such as depreciation, rent, utilities and supervisory and managerial salaries are loaded on to the back of labour and/or material costs through an absorption (or burden) rate.

Perhaps the business uses a standard costing system where expected costs for labour, materials and overheads (known as standards) are established at the start of the year with differences reported throughout the year as variances.

[For a more detailed explanation of some of the alternative methodologies used in calculating and reporting on product or service cost see Chapter 7, Costing.]

Note: EBITDA (Earnings Before Interest, Tax, Depreciation and Amortisation). Whilst this figure does not appear as such in the Profit and Loss Account it is an important component of the Cash Flow Statement and may be calculated and shown as a note or appendix to the Profit and Loss Account.

As explained above, EBIT is another term for Operating Profit.

	£
EBIT	100,000
Depreciation and Amortisation	25,000
EBITDA	125,000

As depreciation and amortisation have already been included in the costs charged against sales in calculating EBIT, they are 'added back' to EBIT to arrive at EBITDA. This is explained in detail on p.51.

INTERPRETING THE NUMBERS
So what does the Profit and Loss Account tell you?

Less than you might think – although it does represent an important aspect of long-term survival; has the market been willing to pay a price for your goods or services that exceeds the cost you've incurred in satisfying those needs?

When you look at a Profit and Loss Account you must remember that Operating Profit is compiled on 'the matching principle' with the sales value being compared to the costs associated with making those sales.

It is neither a comparison of sales against total costs incurred nor is it a statement comparing cash receipts with cash payments.

The value of sales is the total of all the invoices raised during the period – unless you sell everything for cash, this will not be the same as the cash you have received.

Cost is the price of the resources you've consumed in making the products or services that have been sold – the 'attributable' cost. Unless you pay for everything in cash and don't keep any stock this will not be the same as the value of the cheques you've written.

In other words when the accountant is preparing the Profit and Loss Account they are simply looking down the road at what has been sold during the period the statement covers and limiting their questioning to:

- What is the invoiced value of the goods or services that have left the business?
- What costs are tied up in those goods or services that have been sold?
- Hence how much profit has been made?

With their back to the business the statement takes no account of either costs that have been incurred but haven't yet 'gone out on the back of the lorry' (i.e. inventory); neither do they concern themselves with what has been happening to cash.

But the Profit and Loss Account still attempts to provide important information by comparing market prices with the cost to the business of achieving these sales.

By using the matching principle the accountant tries to ensure that by using attributable costs they are comparing 'like with like'.

Take the example of a business that buys in three items and then sells two. If the Profit and Loss Account measured the sales value of the two against the cost of the three the resultant figure would be meaningless. If instead it compares the sales value of the two with the cost of two (the other one sits in the Balance Sheet as inventory), the statement can guide users as to whether the business has organised itself in such a way that the price it can command in the market for its products or services exceeds their cost.

[It is this matching principle that also drives the need for the accountant to prepare "accruals" and "prepayments". Not all bills are received on a monthly basis so when the accountant is preparing the Profit and Loss Account they need to make appropriate adjustments. If utility bills for example are received quarterly in arrears and 'lumps' of utility cost are included in the statement just once a quarter this would distort the picture of what costs the business is really incurring (and hence how much profit they are making) each month. Instead the accountant will include an "accrued" charge each month based on an estimate of the cost of the resources consumed with a small correction made each quarter when the bill comes in and the actual cost is known. Other costs, such as subscriptions, may be payable annually in advance.

In this instance rather than take all the cost in the first month the accountant feeds the cost into the Profit and Loss Account on a monthly basis through a prepayment adjustment.]

The extent to which selling prices have exceeded costs are usually commented on in the context of their "margins". Margins are calculated by measuring profit as a % of sales:

Example: $$\frac{(\text{Selling price} - \text{Cost})}{\text{Selling price}} \times 100\%$$

This may be done by individual product or service or for the business as a whole. Reported margins will depend on where you 'draw the line' on which costs to include in your costing system, and margin comparisons between different product or service lines will be distorted by the extent to which there is cross-subsidisation taking place within the costing system. There are those who would argue therefore that there is little information other than of a very generalised nature on cost, and hence profit, to be gained from the Profit and Loss Account (see Chapter 7, Costing).

If you're looking at a Profit and Loss Account that goes beyond Operating Profit you'll find the cost of interest payments to those who have lent the business money. Borrowing money brings financial risk into the business as interest payments must be made (see p.12) so it is important to look at how easily the business is servicing this cost.

This can be assessed by calculating the Interest Cover – i.e. calculating how many times the interest cost could have been paid out of Operating Profit.

Example: Operating Profit = £100,000
          Interest Costs   £20,000

          Interest Cover =   5

The higher the interest cover the lower the risk. If a business has low *gearing* and high interest cover it is said to have leverage – the potential to borrow more money, if required, at a reasonable rate of interest.

As far as the next step, taxation, is concerned, whilst most businesses (and individuals) try and organise themselves in such a way that they can legitimately minimise their tax liabilities, the amount charged is predominantly driven by government fiscal policy.

The final number to interpret is that of Earnings. One of the key measures businesses use to assess how well they are meeting their shareholders' needs is *Earnings Per Share* (EPS). This measure is calculated by taking the Earnings figure and dividing it by the number of shares in issue and provides a measure (and importantly, over time, a trend) of the 'profit' per share for the owners.

Armed with a Profit and Loss Account and a Balance Sheet you are now able to assess a key part of the management task – how effectively the investment available (as set out in the Balance Sheet) has been used to deliver profit (as measured by Operating Profit). This concept of "profitability" is explained in detail on p.62.

MASTERING PROFIT

All too often when looking for ways to improve the Profit and Loss Account numbers, attention turns to slashing costs.

Don't forget to look for opportunities to improve the top line as well.

Pricing for Profit

It's always very tempting to shave a little off the price to guarantee winning an order – but do your sales team really understand that any discounts come straight off the bottom line?

Look at the impact giving a 1% sales discount has on profit for this business:

| | **Before:** | **After:** |
	£	£
Sales	100,000	99,000
Costs	95,000	95,000
Profit	5,000	4,000

Profit falls by 20%!

Whereas look at the benefit a small increase in selling prices can have:

	Before:	**After:**
	£	£
Sales	100,000	102,000
Costs	95,000	95,000
Profit	5,000	7,000

In this instance a 2% increase in selling prices increases profit by 40%.

And raising your prices might not be as hard as you think.

Check the terms of any sales contracts for escalation clauses and make sure you trigger them when appropriate. It's up to you to do this – your customer is unlikely to remind you!

Make sure that those responsible for agreeing contracts with customers are commercially astute and understand exactly what is included in the price and what should be invoiced as 'extras'. The building industry has a reputation for being good at this. When you're negotiating the contract make sure you also agree the basis for charging any extras then consider invoicing them separately so that if they are challenged, payment for the 'core' work is not delayed.

And while you've got the sales team in your sights, take the opportunity to share with them the benefits to be had of selling additional lines on a customer's order. Look at the costs you incur on activities such as marketing, selling costs, administration and distribution. For many businesses these will not increase if the customer adds an additional item to their basket so the difference between the selling price and the cost of making the product will fall straight to the bottom line. In the service industry, if you've already got someone on-site make sure your team are trained the opportunity to sell that extra service.

In the light of the above, take a look at the way you reward your sales team. Make sure they're motivated to win the 'right' business at the 'right' price.

Managing costs
Now take a look at those costs.
Here's where a few numbers can win people round.

Let's assume times are really tough and your profit margin is perilously tight.

	£
Sales	100,000
Costs	99,000
Profit	1,000

Initially there will inevitably be those who fail to share your enthusiasm to find ways to reduce costs.

"Why bother? If we're only making £1,000 profit and we find ways to reduce costs by 3%, that's an awful lot of angst to go through to increase profit by 3%; that's only an extra £30!"

They're missing the point and you'll miss an opportunity.
   Profit quadruples.

	Before:	After:
	£	£
Sales	100,000	100,000
Costs	99,000	96,000
Profit	1,000	4,000

If you want to make even more impact on your audience show them what happens to the business' *profitability* if you can reduce costs and 'shrink' your investment (see p.65).

Even though you've now convinced everyone of the benefits you may still be wondering where on earth you can find yet more cost savings. You have already 'cracked the whip' over those making the product or delivering the service and can't see how you can get them to work harder. You've tussled with your suppliers and just don't know how you can source any cheaper.

Where is there left to go?

Take a good look around you and you'll find people wasting the company's money. Not because they're lazy but because: firstly, you haven't got your processes organised as effectively as they can be; and secondly, because you don't always get everything right first time. Remember your customer pays a price that rewards you for having best practice and for getting it right. If you choose to have convoluted, resource-consuming processes that's a cost to the business that the customer won't want to pay for. If the way you make things, or the way you deliver the service, or your administration systems are complex and prone to error, you will end up frequently having to 'put things right'. That's another cost the customer isn't willing to bear.

The costs you incur are a consequence of the way you've decided to set out and organise your business. Reflect back on those two categories of investment set out in the Balance Sheet as seen on p.20.

Fixed Assets

When you choose these 'facilities' or 'processes' you lay out the way you intend to run your business for many years into the future. The cost to the business is, for the purposes of the Profit and Loss Account, spread over the asset's useful life to calculate an annual depreciation charge against profit (see appendix 3, Fixed Assets). Depreciation is therefore the cost of the investment you have made in providing your chosen capability to meet market needs and you look to recover this cost through the price the market pays for your products or services. The choices you make will also drive the 'running' costs that you incur – e.g. your choice of equipment will affect maintenance and electricity costs; your choice of premises will affect space costs such as rates and heating.

Once fixed assets have reached the end of what was originally deemed to be their useful life to the business (the period over which they were depreciated) there is no further depreciation charge to be made so continuing to use them may seem a great way to improve profits. But there may be downsides to continuing to use fully depreciated equipment (for example increased maintenance costs, decreased reliability, reduced competitiveness through failure to be able to offer up-to-date technology etc.), and it is this weighing up of the advantages to be had in making new investment against the cost it brings to the business that forms the basis of the *CAPEX* decision. (See Chapter 8, Capital Expenditure Appraisal.)

Working Capital
The way you organise the journey from cash through your business and back into cash again will have implications to the costs that end up in your Profit & Loss Account.

Working Capital Cycle

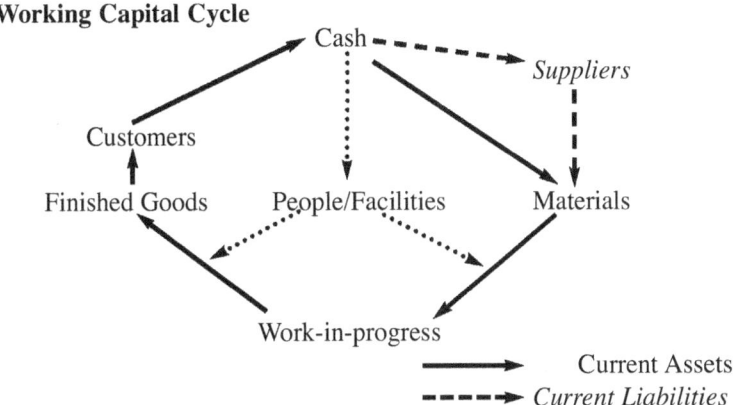

[For a detailed explanation of the cycle see Appendix 4, Working Capital.]

Payables
Your choice of suppliers and the terms and conditions of the purchase orders placed on them will determine not only the price paid but also the costs you incur for carriage inwards, receiving, storage, disposal of packaging etc.

Inventory
The way you organise the speed with which materials come into the business, are transformed into the goods or services the customer wants and are then delivered to them will not only affect the amount of investment you need to keep that working capital cycle turning but will also influence your running costs. Inventory is an asset that you have to look after so you incur handling, storage and security costs. The more inventory you have around, the greater the complexity, so the more you

will spend controlling it (e.g. scheduling, record keeping, stocktaking) and the greater the risk of 'write-offs' (as a result of, for example, inventory losses and obsolescence) – an additional cost to the business that therefore reduces your profit.

Receivables
Whilst you will negotiate as little credit to your customers as you can, unless you've managed to get cash terms (or even better cash upfront), your customer profile will influence the amount of cost you have to incur in collecting payment of your invoices. Do you sell to lots of different customers or just a few? Are your customers local, national or international? How much commercial leverage do you have with them when it comes to making sure they pay on time? Are the necessary checks carried out to make sure your customer is credit-worthy before you take the order? Any bad debts that have to be written off will also reduce your profits.

Remember that costs don't just happen, they are caused by the choices people make. Every time a decision is made there will be cost implications. For effective cost control you therefore need to make sure people understand the financial implications of the choices available to them. Certain decisions may constrain the choices available to the next tier of decision-makers.

Profit by design
Design decisions are a good example of this. Your business is there to serve market needs. Once you've decided which needs you're going to address and the price customers will pay to have them met, you then have to design the product or service that will satisfy those needs. These design decisions are fundamental in determining cost and hence whether you can make a living out of serving that market. For example, the choice of materials you'll use will determine the list of potential suppliers which will then drive not just price and payment terms but the cost you will incur on other aspects such as freight inwards, storage (do you have to buy in bulk?), controlling quality (do they source inspect?), ensuring reliability of supply (do you have to lay in buffer stock?) and administration (can your systems 'speak' to each other?).

As for the costs that will be incurred converting those materials into products, the starting point for determining these will be driven by whether there is in-house capability to do the work required to achieve the design or whether it will need to be sub-contracted out. Then there are the costs of achieving the required level of quality that will stem from the design parameters....

The list of 'knock-on' impacts to cost that originate from the design go on and on. Every line drawn on the designer's easel has £ notes written all over it. Remember that profit is the difference between the selling price and the cost. If the market sets the selling price, your only chance to control your profit is to master those costs. If you treat your designers as 'fluffies', kow-towing to their creative impulses and allowing them to be devoid of any responsibility for cost, you will lose control of your profit.

Margins of Error

You may be surprised that this section hasn't been full of references to "margins" and how to improve them. As explained on p.40, reported margins will depend on where you draw the line in deciding which costs to include in your costing system. In addition, as every costing system has its 'winners and losers', margins may be inappropriate in guiding decisions such as which product or service lines should be expanded and which should be curtailed (see Appendix 9, Product Life-Cycles).

And once you get into the detail of individual product or service margins there's also the danger of the 'cake-cutting farce' wherein instead of trying to reduce the size of the cake (the total costs), energy is wasted on merely trying to cut the slices in different proportions (getting costs reallocated to someone else's product or service).

Just to make matters even worse, reporting on costs is the prime area for using generic terminology in a uniquely 'localised' way!

So, before using any costing information for decision-making purposes it is essential to establish how 'the numbers' have been calculated and therefore their relevance to the matter in hand.

Treat cost 'information' with extreme caution!
Most should come with a business health warning:
"Under no circumstances should these numbers be used in decision-making." (See Chapter 7, Costing.)

4. THE CASH FLOW STATEMENT

INTRODUCTION
Whilst Balance Sheets and Profit and Loss Accounts have been around for hundreds of years, the Cash Flow Statement, as a published document, is a relatively recent development. As explained below, when businesses become more 'sophisticated', profit and cash flow tend to drift apart, and with only the Balance Sheet and Profit and Loss Account to work with, it is less obvious to those reading the accounts when companies are getting into difficulties.

Cash is the lifeblood of the business. You use cash to pay your workforce, pay your suppliers, pay the bank their interest, pay the taxman their dues and pay the shareholders their dividends. Without cash your business grinds to a halt.

But as long as you're making a profit... surely that's enough?

No. Businesses don't fail because they make a loss but because they run out of cash.

You see, once a business:

- takes credit from its suppliers; and/or
- gives credit to its customers; and/or
- does not buy and sell everything the same day (i.e. has inventory); and/or
- purchases facilities or processes (i.e. Fixed Assets)

then TIME has entered the business, so profit and cash flow drift apart.

And not only are profit and cash flow not the same thing, they may not even move in the same direction.

A business can start with cash, make a profit and yet end up at the end of the period with less cash than it started with.

(Conversely a business can start with no cash, make a loss during the period and still end up with more cash than it started with but this isn't a particularly enjoyable or sustainable process.)

Therefore to master the financials you need to run your business in such a way that you don't just make a profit but that you also generate cash.

READING THE CASH FLOW STATEMENT

Cash flow is the difference between cash that has been received and the cash that has been paid out. The Cash Flow Statement shows whether the amount of cash held by the business has increased or decreased during the period and explains why this has happened.

There are different ways in which this statement is presented but whilst the sequence in which items are dealt with varies, the 'building blocks' remain the same.

The starting point, particularly for statements produced for internal use, is usually the amount of profit made during the period – which is why the statement is sometimes referred to as the "Profit to Cash Reconciliation".

In working through the following explanation it will be useful to refer to the example shown overleaf.

Figures in (brackets) are cash outflows:

Cash Flow Statement

	£
Operating Profit	100,000
Depreciation	25,000
EBITDA	125,000
Increase in Inventory	(22,000)
Increase in Receivables	(29,000)
Increase in Payables	8,000
Cash Flow from Operating Activities	82,000
Interest Paid	(20,000)
Tax Paid	(12,000)
Capital Expenditure	(30,000)
Dividends Paid	(28,000)
Increase in Share Capital	3,000
(Decrease) in Cash	(5,000)

Cash Flow from Operating Activities

This is the term that is used to represent the cash flow that has resulted from running the business as distinct from any financing or investment activities. As can be seen from the example above, it considers both cash flowing as a result of Operating Profit and the impact of changing levels of Working Capital.

Operating Profit and Cash Flow

Making a profit (i.e. selling goods or services for more than they cost) is a great way to help bring cash into the business. You will recall from the section on the Profit and Loss Account that there are many different 'levels' of profit but the one usually used to start off the Cash Flow Statement is Operating Profit, also known as EBIT (Earnings Before

Interest and Tax). This is the profit after all the business costs (materials, payroll, expenses, depreciation and amortisation etc.) have been deducted from the sales value but before financing costs such as interest, tax and dividends have been charged.

There is an adjustment to Operating Profit that needs to be made if the Cash Flow Statement is going to eventually explain what has happened to the cash. Take another look at the business costs referred to above. They include depreciation and amortisation. These charges are the accountant's mechanism for being 'fair' in how they calculate profit by spreading the original purchase price of Fixed Assets over their useful life to the business rather than including all the cost in the year of purchase. (See Appendix 3, Fixed Assets). So the depreciation and amortisation charges for the period will have been included as a cost before arriving at Operating Profit. But these charges have nothing to do with cash moving into or out of the business. Cash flowed in the past when the business originally bought and paid for the asset. Nobody pays or receives cash for depreciation or amortisation. Therefore to look at how the business has performed from a 'cash' perspective the accountant has to 'add back' those depreciation and amortisation charges to EBIT thereby effectively restating the profit to a level 'higher up' the Profit and Loss Account – EBITDA (Earnings Before Interest, Tax, Depreciation and Amortisation).

[Depreciation and amortisation may also be referred to as "Non cash expenses". There may be other such expenses where the cost has been included in the Profit and Loss Account but where there are no cash flow implications (e.g. creating a provision for future warranty claims) and the statement will need to adjust for these as well.]

Working Capital and Cash Flow

Once the adjustment to EBIT has been made to arrive at EBITDA, the next items in the statement address the impact of the constrained perspective the accountant has in calculating profit. Take another look at that picture on p.38. Profit is the difference between the sales value of the goods invoiced during the period and the cost of the resources consumed in enabling the business to make and deliver the goods that have been sold.

It is important to note the following:

- Profit considers just the cost of the goods or services sold – not the costs incurred
- Profit looks at sales invoices – not cash receipts
- Profit looks at costs – not cash payments

To move to a 'cash' perspective, adjustments therefore have to be made for the following.

The increase or decrease in inventory

Carrying out this adjustment converts the "cost of goods and services sold" in the Profit and Loss Account into the "costs incurred" during the period regardless of whether they relate to goods or services that have been sold or are still held in inventory and will be invoiced in a future period.

If the inventory value has increased then you must have incurred more costs than just those that have found their way into the Profit and Loss Account.

Conversely if the inventory value has decreased then the costs you have incurred will be less than the costs included in your Profit and Loss Account.

The increase or decrease in receivables

By allowing for this the "sales" figure included in the Profit and Loss Account is converted to "cash receipts".

The increase or decrease in payables

Adjusting for this increase or decrease converts "costs incurred" into "cash payments".

[If you want to work through an example of these working capital adjustments they are included in the worked example in Appendix 6.]

Interest and Tax

The statement shows the amount of Interest and Tax paid – note this may be different to the figures charged in the Profit and Loss Account due to the timing of payments.

Capital Expenditure

Having adjusted the profit figure for the accountant's depreciation charge to take it out of a statement concerned with inflows and outflows of cash (see above), the next step is to include the cost of any Capital Expenditure (CAPEX) during the period as this is the point at which cash really does flow.

Dividends

The statement shows the dividends paid which may be different to the figures shown in the supplementary statement to the Profit and Loss Account due to the timing of payments.

Financing Activities

The statement also sets out the cash flow resulting from increases or decreases in long-term finance (e.g. share capital and loans).

A worked example of the Cash Flow Statement is provided in Appendix 6.

INTERPRETING THE CASH FLOW STATEMENT

Take another look at that complete statement on p.50.

As few people within an organisation play a key role in decisions on how the business is financed (and as cash flow problems can not be perpetually resolved by just bringing in additional capital), it makes sense to focus on the areas most people can influence.

We are therefore left with what can be referred to as the '5 levers' to generate cash in a business.

> EBITDA
> + Movement in Working Capital:
> Δ Inventory
> Δ Receivables
> Δ Payables
> + <u>Capital Expenditure</u>
> = Cash Flow
>
> *Note: Δ means 'the increase or decrease in'*

Remember that this is not the accountant's complete cash flow as it only includes those items that are under the control of local managers and therefore need to be 'mastered'.

EBITDA
This is Operating Profit (or EBIT) adjusted to exclude the impact of any charges for depreciation and amortisation – see p.51. EBITDA is generated by selling goods or services to the market at a price that exceeds their cost.

Movement in Working Capital
Increases or decreases in the elements of working capital will have an effect on cash flow.

- If inventory increases this is 'bad' for cash.
- If receivables increase this is 'bad' for cash.
- If, however, payables increase this is 'good' for cash.

If you're unsure of why this is, look at the Working Capital cycle explained in detail in Appendix 4.

Every time the cycle 'swells' (because the business holds more inventory or allows customers more credit or takes less credit from suppliers), cash is 'sucked into' the cycle. On the other hand when the cycle is 'squeezed' (by holding less inventory or allowing customers less credit or taking more credit from suppliers) cash is released.

Capital Expenditure
This is the amount spent on new facilities or processes in the period.

From the above adjustments you can see why profit and cash flow will not have the same value (unless coincidently all the items in the middle net out to zero); neither will they necessarily even move in the same direction.

If the business makes a profit but the other levers head in the 'wrong' direction then cash flow may be negative.

If the business makes a loss but 'good' things happen elsewhere on the statement then cash flow could still be positive.

Examples:

	£	£
EBITDA	10,000	(10,000)
Movement in Working Capital:		
Δ Inventory	(2,000)	4,000
Δ Receivables	(6,000)	9,000
Δ Payables	1,000	(1,000)
Capital Expenditure	(5,000)	nil
Cash inflow/(outflow)	(2,000)	2,000

So should you always expect to be able to get 100% "cash conversion" (i.e. see all your EBITDA flowing down to the cash flow line)?

It very much depends on what is going on in your business at the time.

Ironically businesses tend to be at their most vulnerable, from a cash perspective, when they're successful as increasing volumes of cash are flowing out before they start to flow in again.

On the other hand, if there is a downturn in activity and the warning signs are spotted and acted on promptly, cash may well flow in as Working Capital is 'ratcheted down' and Capital Expenditure put on hold.

[For more information on the impact of product life-cycles on cash flow, see Appendix 9.]

MASTERING CASH FLOW

To master cash flow you must set about managing and controlling the '5 levers' referred to above.

EBITDA

Forget the jargon and think "profit".

Nobody manages cash flow by thinking about depreciation or amortisation. Focus instead on how you can improve your profits.

Whilst you don't necessarily have to start with a profit to generate cash it makes life much easier and infinitely more pleasant if you do!

If you're making losses then the only way you can keep the cash flowing in is to 'shrink' the business, reducing the investment in working capital and reining back on capital expenditure – or continually bringing in additional finance which will become both increasingly difficult to find and expensive when you do.

You make a profit by selling your goods or services into a market at a price that exceeds the cost. It is important therefore that you've clearly identified the market you are serving and have aligned your business to that market so that you can meet those needs as efficiently and effectively as possible. Customers do not pay a price premium to charitably support inefficient suppliers. Gone (for most businesses) are the days of "cost plus" pricing where the price would be determined by an agreed mark-up on whatever it cost you to provide those goods or services. The market sets the price according to the value it places on the product or service you are providing. You should be doing everything you can to 'position' your offering in the marketplace in such a way that you can command the highest price possible (by the quality and reliability of your products or services, your excellent supportive relationship with your customer etc.) but ultimately you don't set the price; the market does.

But that does not mean you abdicate all financial responsibility as to whether you make a profit or not.

Whilst the market may set the selling price, you determine the cost by the way you go about your business. Take a look at p.41 (Mastering Profit) for some ideas on how to get the EBITDA you deserve.

Movement in Working Capital

Take another look at that Working Capital cycle on p.45.
Remember, you're looking for ways to 'squeeze' rather than 'swell' the investment.

Inventory

If inventory is an asset why do you want to get rid of it?

Not only because for every asset there is an equivalent liability (e.g. the money you had to borrow from the bank to finance it) and because it requires you to incur additional costs (e.g. handling and storage), but also because it's a risky way to tie up your money.

As soon as you embark on your journey around the cycle and move out of cash you bring risk to the business:

- What happens if you buy the wrong inventory?

- What happens if there's a modification to your product or the way you deliver your service so that the inventory is no longer required?
- What if there's a change in the market making the inventory obsolete?

Your aim must be to whiz through the cycle as fast as you can holding as little inventory as possible, consistent with keeping your customer happy. And there's the rub.

There is only one person who brings the cash into your business.
Your customer. So it's vital that you can give him what he wants when he wants it. The only reason for holding inventory is because it's the only way you can work within the order leadtime your customer is willing to accept. So, every time you reduce the leadtime it takes to produce your goods or services the less inventory you will need to hold.

What determines your leadtime?
The market should have determined your product or service specification (after all you should be meeting their needs, no more, no less) but it's down to you how you've decided to produce it – and the design decision is critical here.

The answers to these questions will start you thinking about what is driving your leadtime:

- Which suppliers do you use?
- Can you negotiate consignment stock with them?
- Have you looked carefully at the 'cost' of volume discounts (e.g. additional initial investment, handling, and storage)?
- Do you do all the work yourself or do you use sub-contractors?
- How efficiently does the work flow through the process?
- Are there 'bottlenecks'?
- Are some tasks difficult and prone to result in scrap or rework requiring you to hold buffer stock just-in-case?

But before you empty the shelves be careful. Understand your market. In some markets availability is paramount. If you supply critical components for oil-drilling equipment the customer will send a helicopter to collect the part. Because of the cost of downtime to the customer, the price you charge is secondary to the importance of having that part on the shelf. Therefore, in this case you may align yourself with your market by holding substantial inventory (although even then not more than you need!) – but you will, of course, have made sure that the prices you can charge will reward you for the investment you have had to make and the additional risk you have therefore had to take.

Receivables

- Is your business sales-driven?
- Is there a 'get-it-out-the-door' mentality?
- Do you have a hockey stick*?

[*This is when, instead of a nice steady stream of sales throughout the month, very little happens in the first week or two, things gradually pick up in week 3 and then the vast majority of sales happen in the last few days of the month. Picture the daily sales graph and it has the shape of a hockey stick.]

If you have any (or all) of these, in the chaos that surrounds month end, shipping and invoicing mistakes will happen, making the payment difficult to collect. Think about what happens to your business's finances when you make a sale. All you do is move your money into someone else's warehouse. There's no real financial benefit to your business until the customer pays you and, until he does, your cash is still at risk. Therefore, you want to make sure that everyone in the team understands that the job isn't finished until the customer pays.

If you can make cash sales, that's great (as are progress payments if you can get them). But where customers expect credit, salespeople need to ensure that just like price, this is a matter for negotiation.

Every time salespeople allow your customers credit it means cash is tied up in receivables. Not only is additional investment required to finance this but there is also additional risk.

- What happens if the customer won't pay?
- What happens if the customer goes under before he pays?

- What happens if you've overstretched yourself financially by taking on a large order so that you can't pay your bills in the meantime?

Whose job is it to collect the cash from customers?
Everyone in the business. This critical step in the cash flow journey has to be managed professionally.

You can't collect money where there isn't an invoice.
Check your processes to make sure there are no 'shortcuts' allowing goods or services to be delivered without invoices being raised. If you've negotiated a contract with stage-payments make sure those involved understand what those trigger-points are and that the invoices are raised promptly.

Customers won't pay if they didn't place an order.
It's often said that "everyone works for the customer" – but in that case they need to be paid! Beware of the rush to 'help a customer out' where costs are incurred before the order is received.

You can't collect on an invoice where there isn't a price.
Once again, in the desire to be helpful, businesses expose themselves to grave risks by commencing work on a TBA (to be agreed) basis. This is particularly risky (and you put yourself at a severe commercial disadvantage in subsequent negotiations) in the case of services where, once performed, they cannot be 'returned', and customer-specific products where there is no alternative customer for the goods.

You can't collect if it isn't due...
Credit terms need to be clear and understood. Whilst "Net 30" means payment 30 days after invoice date, "Net monthly" means payment is due on the last day of the month following the one in which the invoice is dated – so that could mean up to an extra month's credit for your customer. If you're involved with shipping goods overseas it's especially important to get advice on the precise meaning of the various terms used.

... but you can 'nurse' it through the system!

It's important to establish good working relationships with your customers – and not just with the buyers. Don't wait for invoices to become overdue. If your customer is strapped for cash and is deciding which suppliers to pay you want to make sure you make the cut. By understanding your customer's payment authorisation processes and the people involved in that flow, you can progress your invoice through the system ensuring it has been 'signed off' and is ready for payment well before the due date.

Payables

You might think the advice is going to be to take as much credit from your suppliers as you can get away with by ignoring any agreed payment terms and stringing them along for as long as possible.

It isn't. If you're going to set up your business in such a way that you can race through the Working Capital cycle as fast as you can and at minimum cost, you're going to need good relationships with carefully selected suppliers. Price matters as do negotiated payment terms (particularly if your customers are looking for long credit periods from you). But so do quality, lead time and reliability of supply. Remember that whilst taking additional credit from your supply chain improves your cash flow, having to lay in buffer stocks to protect yourself against being placed on 'stop' does the opposite. And it doesn't stop there:

- What about the additional costs you incur by playing one supplier off against another?
- Who has to take time out to deal with irate phone calls from unpaid suppliers?
- What if your failure to pay pushes your supplier over the edge and into liquidation? What will it cost you to approve another supplier?
- What is the cost of disrupted production?
- Will you end up paying for overtime and premium transport costs if you're still to fulfil your customer's order on time?

All these costs go against profit, therefore reducing your EBITDA. Another blow to cash flow.

So the message is to take the negotiation of credit terms seriously with your suppliers. Make sure that your buyers understand that the longer the credit period the less cash you have to find to keep your Working Capital cycle turning. But they must be terms your supplier can afford. If not, you may end up paying him earlier anyway just to keep him afloat. Once you've agreed terms, keep your word.

Capital Expenditure

When businesses carry out Capital Expenditure (i.e. the purchase of Fixed Assets) they are investing their money now in assets that they believe will bring value to the business for more than one financial year. That's why, when it comes to calculating profit, the accountant spreads the purchase price over the asset's useful life by charging a 'fair' amount (i.e. depreciation) against profit each year.

But whilst from a profit perspective the costs are spread, it's not what is happening to the cash. The cash flows out of the business in the year of purchase. The challenge is to make sure you buy the 'right' Fixed Assets. If you've aligned yourself correctly with your market and have set yourself up to make the products or services the market needs in the most cost-effective way using the most appropriate processes, the market will reward you for your investment in the price it pays for your goods or services. That's good for EBITDA and hence good for cash.

However, purchasing Fixed Assets is a risky business because you have to spend the cash now in expectation of that stream of profit (and cash) in the future. [For more discussion on the approaches taken to evaluate CAPEX requests see Chapter 8.]

5. FINANCIAL RATIOS AND OTHER MEASURES OF PERFORMANCE

INTRODUCTION

Numbers taken in isolation may mean very little.

Is a monthly sales figure of £200,000 'good' or 'bad'? Without something to compare it with (e.g. a forecast or last month's figure) there is little that can be said.

Sometimes other financial figures are needed to form a view.

Is an inventory value of £50,000 too high or too low? If you knew the average value of goods or services shipped per month, you could get a better picture by restating the information as a "number of days inventory".

Even then, without knowledge of the kind of business you were looking at, it would be hard to comment. 30 days inventory may be a great achievement for certain types of manufacturing businesses but to a volume retailer, who plans to turn their inventory over every few days, it would be a disaster.

Therefore you need to take care when reviewing ratios or performance measures to look at them in the context of the business and also focus more on ratios and trends rather than absolute values.

You can take any two numbers and use them to create a ratio but for it to be meaningful there must be an inter-relationship that you are trying to master. Businesses tend to evolve their own variants but here are some of the most common.

Profitability (Return on Capital Employed)

If you were to be offered the opportunity to invest in a venture that guaranteed you a profit of £1,000 next year would you be interested?

Setting aside questions of legality and trust, the most important question you would want answered is, "How much would I have to invest?"

If it was £10,000, and a 10% return was better than you could make elsewhere, you might be tempted. If on the other hand you were told you would have to invest £1,000,000 you'd walk away.

What matters to you is therefore not profit but profitability, i.e. how much profit you make relative to how much had to be invested to earn that profit.

In businesses profitability is usually measured as Return on Capital Employed (ROCE), which is expressed as a % and calculated as follows:

$$\text{ROCE} = \frac{\text{Operating Profit}}{\text{Net Capital Employed}} \times 100\%$$

Operating Profit (also known as EBIT) is the profit after all business operating costs have been met but before any financing costs. It is also commonly referred to as "the bottom line" because it is often seen to be the lowest point on the Profit and Loss Account over which local management have control and therefore accountability (see p.36).

Net Capital Employed (NCE) is the total of long-term finance invested in the business both from shareholders (*Net Worth*) and from lenders (*Loans*) and is shown on the bottom half of the Balance Sheet as presented on p.21.

Using the figures from the Profit and Loss Account on p.35 and the Balance Sheet on p.21:

$$\text{ROCE} = \frac{\text{Operating Profit}}{\text{Net Capital Employed*}} \times 100\% = \frac{£100,000}{£500,000} \times 100\% = 20\%$$

[*Note that as the Balance Sheet balances, Net Capital Employed (how much has been made available to invest) equals *Net Assets Employed* (where that investment has been made – i.e. *Fixed Assets* plus *Working Capital*).]

ROCE therefore sums up a key aspect of management's task. Given the amount of investment at their disposal (NCE), how effectively have they used this to firstly, through their CAPEX decisions, set out what they can offer the market in terms of business capability (Fixed Assets) and secondly organise the way the business will operate (Working Capital), in order to make and deliver products or services on which they can make an Operating Profit?

Encapsulating aspects of both the Balance Sheet and the Profit and Loss Account, this ratio might seem a little difficult to get to grips with. To master the ratio it's helpful to break it down into two parts using 'the multiplier'. Introduce Sales (from the Profit and Loss Account) into the top and bottom of the ratio as follows:

$$\text{ROCE} = \frac{\text{Operating Profit}}{\text{NCE}} \times 100\%$$

$$= \frac{\text{Operating Profit}}{\text{Sales}} \times 100\% \quad \mathbf{X} \quad \frac{\text{Sales}}{\text{NCE}}$$

[Remember that when you multiply two ratios together you can 'cancel out' the two Sales figures ending up with the original ratio.]

As the Sales figure in the example was £1,000,000 (see p.35) the ratio becomes:

$$\text{ROCE} = \frac{£100,000}{£1,000,000} \times 100\% \quad \mathbf{X} \quad \frac{£1,000,000}{£500,000}$$

$$= 10\% \quad \mathbf{X} \quad 2$$

$$= 20\%$$

$\frac{\text{Operating Profit}}{\text{Sales}} \times 100\%$ is the Profit Margin and in this example is 10%

As you have seen on p.63, Net Capital Employed (NCE) equals Net Assets Employed (NAE) so:

$$\frac{Sales}{NCE} = \frac{Sales}{NAE}$$

$\frac{Sales}{NAE}$ is known as Asset Turn and in this instance is 2.

Therefore: ROCE = Profit Margin **X** Asset Turn.

So if you can improve either your Profit Margin or your Asset Turn – or, better still, for a 'multiplied' benefit, both – you will improve profitability.

Mastering the Profit Margin
There are two ways to improve your margin.
You can either increase your sales without proportionately increasing your costs and/or you can eliminate unnecessary costs from the business.

Increasing your sales might involve selling more products or services – but it could be a simple matter of making sure you're pricing your sales appropriately and including everything you're entitled to on your invoice.

If you can add an extra 1% to your invoices (noting that this increase also increases your Operating Profit) then profitability, using the above example, increases from 20% to 22% as shown below:

Sales increases from £1,000,000 to £1,010,000
Operating Profit increases from £100,000 to £110,000

$$ROCE = \frac{Operating\ Profit}{Sales} \times 100\% \; \mathbf{X} \; \frac{Sales}{NAE}$$

$$= \frac{£110,000}{£1,010,000} \times 100\% \; \mathbf{X} \; \frac{£1,010,000}{£500,000}$$

$$= 11\% \quad \mathbf{X} \quad 2$$

$$= 22\%$$

As far as eliminating costs are concerned, motivate waste-reduction activities by demonstrating the substantial impact on profit margins (and therefore ROCE) of a relatively small saving in cost.

Using the figures as before:

Sales are £1,000,000 and as your Operating Profit is £100,000 your costs must be £900,000.

If you can reduce your costs by 3% (£27,000) then Operating Profit increases to £127,000.

Your calculation of ROCE then becomes:

$$\text{ROCE} = \frac{\text{Operating Profit}}{\text{Sales}} \times 100\% \quad \mathbf{X} \quad \frac{\text{Sales}}{\text{NAE}}$$

$$= \frac{£127,000}{£1,000,000} \times 100\% \quad \mathbf{X} \quad \frac{£1,000,000}{£500,000}$$

$$= 12.7\% \quad \mathbf{X} \quad 2$$

$$= 25.4\%$$

Mastering the Asset Turn

This ratio measures how well you are 'working' your assets to generate sales. Once again there are two ways to improve your Asset Turn.

One is to increase Sales without proportionately increasing your investment in Fixed Assets and Working Capital.

The other is to maintain your value of Sales whilst releasing unnecessary investment in the business by rationalising those Fixed Assets and squeezing that *Working Capital cycle*.

The benefits to be derived from increasing your Sales have been referred to above. Now consider how to challenge that investment.

Fixed Assets

Fixed Assets are purchased through the *CAPEX* decision and are frequently justified on the basis of the additional sales they will bring to the business. Therefore the relationship between the 'offering' of capability made to the market through the investment in Fixed Assets and the success that brings in terms of winning orders for the business is tracked through the Fixed Asset Turn.

$$\text{Fixed Asset Turn} = \frac{\text{Sales}}{\text{Fixed Assets}}$$

To master this ratio you need to make sure that your business gets the CAPEX decision right (see Chapter 8) and then markets this capability successfully.

Working Capital
The ratios used to scrutinise Working Capital will vary between businesses but typically you will find:

$$\frac{\text{Working Capital*}}{\text{Sales}} \times 100\%$$

*This will usually exclude Cash

The aim is to reduce this % by mastering its constituent parts of Inventory, Receivables and Payables.

Inventory
Inventory investment is usually expressed as a number of days' inventory or through inventory turns – i.e. the number of times the inventory is 'turned' in a year.

$$\frac{\text{Inventory}}{\text{Average daily Sales}} = \text{No. days inventory}$$

[*Note* that as it is unlikely that your inventory will be held in exactly the right proportions for your sales, this will not be the number of days you could survive if you 'turned the tap off' and stopped all deliveries from suppliers.]

Some businesses will calculate average daily sales looking backwards, whilst others will make the ratio more meaningful by looking forwards using the sales forecast.

Instead of using average daily Sales, some businesses may try to make the absolute figure more realistic by using average daily Cost of Sales which also removes the susceptibility of the ratio to changes in pricing, and alleviates the impact of changes in the sales mix.

Inventory turn, the number of times stock is 'turned over' in a year is:

$$\frac{365*}{\text{No. days inventory}}$$

*Some companies use the number of working days per annum.

If appropriate these ratios may be analysed further into different categories of inventory e.g. raw materials, work-in-progress (WIP) and finished goods.

Inventory ties money up and brings risk to the business.
Check how the inventory ratio is calculated in your business. Remember you want inventory days to be going down or inventory turn going up!
You don't master inventory by focusing on inventory values. The amount of inventory you're holding is a consequence of the way you've designed and organised production of your products or services. The only reason for holding inventory is that without it you are unable to meet your customers' needs in an acceptable timescale.
Therefore, the faster you can move through the process of bringing in materials and then getting them out through the door as finished goods or services to satisfy a customer order the better.

Receivables
Receivables investment is usually measured in "debtor days". Remember that even when your goods and services have been invoiced and sold to your customers, there's no real financial benefit to you until you've collected the cash. The extent to which you are mastering this last step of the cash-generating Working Capital cycle is calculated as follows:

$$\text{Debtor Days} = \frac{\text{Receivables}}{\text{Average Daily Sales}}$$

As the receivables figure relates to sales that have already been made, the appropriate sales figure to use here is one that looks backwards rather than forwards.

Your aim is to have the lowest number of days you can.

Further information is usually provided in the form of an "Aged Receivables Report" which analyses the total receivables figures into the value of invoices that are not yet due and those that are overdue.

Overdues are then analysed according to the extent to which payment is late – e.g. under 30 days, 30-60 days, 60 days+.

To comply with the principle of prudency (see p.26) businesses have to make a provision for "bad debts" covering those invoices over which there is some uncertainty that payment will eventually be made. This may be done by providing for all invoices overdue by, say, 60 days.

Whilst making a provision effectively 'writes off' these debts as far as valuing assets for the Balance Sheet is concerned, this is merely a question of prudency – there should never be any question over your continued determination to be paid!

For further pointers on how to master the collection of debts see p.58.

Payables

Payables allows you to finance some of your inventory (and possibly even your receivables) using your suppliers' money. To monitor the extent to which you are using the credit negotiated with your supply chain, you can calculate your Creditor Days:

$$\text{Creditor Days} = \frac{\text{Payables}}{\text{Average Daily Purchases}}$$

This rather broad brush ratio may be of limited use if credit terms vary between suppliers.

There are many variants of these Working Capital ratios.

To master them, understand how they are calculated and the influence your actions have on them. Make sure the ratios are calculated on a consistent basis and then assess your success by looking at the trend rather than the absolutes.

Liquidity Ratios

Liquidity is about having enough cash when you need it. A "liquid" asset is cash or something that can be turned into cash quickly.

Text book ratios include the following:

Current Ratio

$$\frac{\text{Current Assets}}{\text{Current Liabilities}} = \frac{\text{Inventory + Receivables + Cash}}{\text{Trade Creditors* and other short-term debt}}$$

*Amounts owed to suppliers

This calculates the 'cover' provided by the *Current Assets* for the short-term debts as shown in the *Current Liabilities*.

Acid Test Ratio

$$\frac{\text{Current Assets - Inventory}}{\text{Current Liabilities}}$$

This more stringent measure excludes inventory on the grounds that it is not considered to be a liquid asset as it takes time firstly to turn it into a saleable item and secondly for the invoice to progress through receivables and arrive eventually as cash.

For liquidity measures to have any meaning, you have to understand the nature of the business and the 'timescales' attached to each part of the Working Capital flow.

Inventory may be a liquid asset to a retailer with rapid turnover on their shelves and where customers pay in cash but not to a business with lengthy contracts on which there are no stage-payments.

Receivables may be considered to be a liquid asset if typical credit terms to customers are a matter of days but not if they are a matter of months.

When looking at the Current Liabilities the important point to ascertain is when these debts will fall due. Your material suppliers may have negotiated to give you 60 days credit but some of those other debts may have very different terms.

Use your knowledge to answer the key question.

Does your business have, or will it have, sufficient cash to meet its obligations as and when they fall due?

***

Gearing

Gearing provides an assessment of financial risk by measuring the proportion of long-term funding provided by lenders (Loans) against that provided by shareholders. The amount provided by the shareholders, known as Net Worth or Shareholders' Funds, comprises both the Share Capital and the Reserves (i.e. profits left over for shareholders that have been reinvested back into the business rather than taken out as dividends) – see p.23.

Gearing is calculated in a number of ways including:

$$\frac{\text{Loans}}{\text{Net Worth}}$$

or:

$$\frac{\text{Loans}}{\text{Net Capital Employed *}}$$

* i.e. Net Worth plus Loans

In both cases, the higher the gearing the greater the financial risk as loans have to be serviced (i.e. interest paid) regardless of how well the business has performed whereas shareholders, as the owners and hence risk-takers, have no such guarantees (see p.12).

Of course if you can organise your business so that you can continue to keep the customer happy whilst driving excess investment out of your Fixed Assets and Working Capital, you're going to be able to reduce the amount of long-term funding you need.

If you do this by repaying some of your loans you'll not only reduce that gearing but also reduce your interest costs thereby improving your profit.

Take a look again at all those fixed assets and working capital. Are you sure there's nothing else you can 'squeeze'?

***

Earnings per share (EPS)

The shareholders own the business and therefore earn whatever is left over after all the business costs have been met. This figure is referred to as Earnings. (Some of these earnings will be taken out as dividends with the rest being reserved for reinvestment back into the business.)

$$\text{Earnings Per Share} = \frac{\text{Earnings}}{\text{No. of shares}}$$

EPS therefore reflects the 'profit' earned on each share and will be used by shareholders to assess the performance of the business in using their investment effectively.

To improve the earnings you need to maximise your sales, whilst minimising both your operational and, (by minimising the amount of investment you need to finance those fixed assets and working capital,) your financing costs.

To do this you need to:

- make sure you understand your customers' needs and that you design your offering to meet those needs. No more and no less;
- ensure you attract as much revenue as you can from meeting those needs;
- align your business capability with the market so that you produce your goods or services at a minimum cost; (see Appendix 3, Fixed Assets.)
- maximise the speed through which products or services flow through that capability; (see Appendix 4, Working Capital.)
- have a 'right first time' approach that minimises wasted time and materials.

***

Measures of Performance

You might be in business to make money, but that doesn't mean that every performance measure needs to have a £ note attached to it.

Making money is about supplying goods and services to the market at a price that exceeds the business costs.

All the costs, including financing costs.

So it's quite simple. You want to sell as much as you can at minimum cost and with minimum investment, and internal measures of performance need to monitor how you well you are doing this.

What should you measure to become more competitive?

Imagine you've decided to enter a marathon and before embarking on a challenging fitness programme, you go to your doctor for a health-check. You are a mass of complex biological processes. The doctor cannot possibly measure everything so he selects a key group of measures to assess how fit you are now and what areas you can work on to improve your fitness and hence your competitiveness. He might measure blood pressure, cholesterol levels, do a simple blood test, check your BMI …

It's just the same with companies.

Look at your business. There is a mass of activities going on and it would be crazy to try to measure everything. So you need to find a balanced group of measures that can 'paint the picture' of what is going on, tell you how you are performing, indicate opportunities for improvement and provide an early warning when things start to go awry.

This is where internal measures of performance (MOPS), often referred to as Key Performance Indicators (KPIs) or "metrics", come in. Ever mindful of the need to eliminate unnecessary costs to the business they should use data that is easily captured, be simple to calculate, provide rapid feedback and be readily understood. Visual displays such as graphs can help.

Some of these metrics will be obviously financial, whilst others may not appear to be so. Look again. You should be able to find the link.

Every metric should be capturing an aspect of your business' performance in doing more with less. And that's how you make money.

However, just as you should be careful what you wish for, you should be careful what you measure.

You get what you measure. What gets measured gets managed.

So not only do you need to check that you're measuring the right things, you also need to ensure a holistic approach to improving your performance.

Go back to the example of your preparations for the marathon. If the doctor told you that the only thing preventing you from putting in a world-class performance was that you needed to lose weight, what would happen? You'd just focus on shedding those kilograms to the detriment of other aspects of your training regime and end up less competitive than when you started.

It's just the same with metrics.

If you measure someone just on their ability to say reduce inventory levels they'll achieve them – but you'll probably have some aggrieved customers when, with shortages, you fail to deliver on time.

Measure solely on on-time delivery and you'll need another warehouse to store products on a just-in-case basis.

Push for purchasing savings and you'll end up with stacks of surplus materials bought in bulk at 'bargain prices'.

Select your metrics carefully to achieve that balance.

And once you've chosen those metrics make sure you communicate clearly to everyone how the decisions they take contribute to each of the measures. So if, for example, you're measuring inventory turn you need to make clear that that's not just down to the people in operations; others including designers and the teams in sales and purchasing all have roles to play.

Some businesses follow this up to the extent of having a series of departmental or even personal metrics cascaded down from the 'top-level' business metrics through a process called "policy deployment". In this instance whilst the despatch manager's contribution to improving inventory turn might be assessed by measuring the average time taken to ship finished products, the salesperson's metrics may include a measure of the reliability of their sales forecasts.

6. BUDGETING

INTRODUCTION

What is it about the word "budget" that causes people to panic?

Rather than being delighted on receiving the news that they're now going to be responsible for setting and managing their own budget, many feel overwhelmed and ill-equipped for doing so.

Forget the budget for a moment. Can you plan your activities and those for the people around you and monitor how you're all doing, taking corrective action where required? Then you've already mastered the difficult part of the task. The only bit you're missing is attaching a financial valuation to those plans – and that's the easy part.

All budgeting and budgetary control involves is preparing plans, attaching £ notes to them, using information prepared by your accountant on a regular basis (usually monthly) to check your progress against those plans and taking any appropriate corrective action.

THE BIG PLAN

It's important that the budgeting process starts at the top level with a 'team plan'.

A football club may have the 11 most talented individuals on the pitch but, without agreement on the goalmouth into which the team are intending to shoot, the tactics they're going to use and the position each player is going to play, they will not end up with the best team performance.

It's just the same in your business. You may have the best sales people in the world, an outstanding production team, expert buyers and a design capability second to none. But if there's not a clear understanding of the market opportunity the business is targeting, the products or services that are to be designed to meet those needs and how these are to be produced, there will be chaos.

Salespeople will sell anything and make promises to customers that can't possibly be met.

Designers will come up with fantastic products for which there are no markets (or markets in which the value placed on the product or service is far less than the costs that would be incurred in producing them).

Buyers will bring in large quantities of materials on which they have negotiated fantastic discounts – but that nobody actually needs.

And as for those in production? Caught in the middle with customers screaming for products or services that at best can't be delivered in the timescale promised (and at worst don't exist) they'll just keep making anything (and often on overtime) just to hit those production targets.

There has to be a better way.

It starts at the top. Your business exists to make money. How are you going to do that? Businesses need to understand their markets so that they can identify the opportunities that they're going to exploit. Making money means you need to sell products or services into markets where the value customers place on having their needs met exceeds the cost you're going to incur in making them.

This needs careful planning and there need to be timescales attached to these plans. Most businesses will make detailed plans for the next financial year but these should be an integrated part of a longer-term vision ensuring the seeds are sown for future years where appropriate by, for example, investing in research, developing new markets and investing in new technology.

The next step is to identify the limiting factor. In most companies this is the amount of business you believe you can win – i.e. the sales forecast. In some instances the limiting factor may be something else, for example, the availability of personnel with a particular skill, the ability to source certain raw materials or the capacity of the equipment.

(While this limiting factor might constrain the business' ability to make money in the short-term, it should feature right at the top of the 'to-do' list as it identifies what is holding the business back.

Opportunities should be sought to shift the constraint to the right by, for example, identifying new markets, cross-training, redesigning products or services and *CAPEX*.)

Now the top-level plan is in place it needs to be cascaded down through the business so that everyone can work what out what they will need to do (and therefore how much it will cost) to achieve their part of the plan. As there will only be limited resources available, this needs to be done in a way that tries to ensure that resources are allocated in the best interests of the business.

That's where the budgets come in.

MAKING IT WORK

Once all budget holders have worked out how they are going to achieve their part of the plan and therefore the budgets they will require, these budgets are then added up to see what 'the numbers' would look like if the plan were achieved and therefore whether the plan is acceptable.

To do this a forecast Profit and Loss Account, Balance Sheet and Cash Flow Statement are prepared together with forecast key ratios. Almost inevitably the result will be unacceptable on the first attempt so budgets will need to be re-examined and the process repeated until the plan is acceptable and the budgets can be approved. Even then there may be a further iterative loop to pass through if the final forecast has to be signed off by a higher authority such as head office.

These revisions to budgets can be fraught with difficulty if either due to the pressure of time or a general lack of co-operation from budget-holders, accountants end up slashing budgets to 'fix' the numbers.

Inconsistencies result where, for example, sales forecasts are maintained whilst packaging costs are cut without any rationale as to how such savings are to be made.

A complete lack of ownership then follows making budgetary control difficult to enforce. And next year, budget holders, wary of a repeat of indiscriminate budget-chopping, pad their budgets in anticipation and the process degenerates into a game of poker rather than a rational attempt to allocate scarce resources to where they can be used most effectively.

Once the forecast is agreed the process of budgetary control can begin. Actual expenditure is measured against the budget to check progress against the plan. Where spending is not in line with the plan, there needs to be action. This may be to carry out 'corrective action' to get back in line with the budget or to send a message up the line to say that the plan needs to be revised.

MASTERING YOUR BUDGET
Setting the budget
All too often there is a tendency to work back-to-front with a 'This is what I want, this is what I'm going to do with it, therefore this is what you'll get' mentality. Start at the beginning, not the end.

Step 1: The reason you need a budget is that you have a role to play in achieving the team plan. There is a job for you to do. Understand what that job is, the level of performance required, and the timescale in which it needs to be achieved.

Step 2: Use your expertise to examine the options and then decide what is the most appropriate way of achieving your part of the plan.

Step 3: List down the resources you'll need: people, services, equipment, materials...

Step 4: Attach financial values to that list – and the accountant should be well-equipped to help you with this stage.

It's helpful, once you've prepared your budget, to have a session with someone who will challenge what you've come up with – not to be difficult but to give you the chance to reflect on the process and ensure you can justify the assumptions and choices you have made. A fresh pair of eyes might also spot that glaring omission or inconsistency.

Note that the more thought you've put into the process the better you are able to defend yourself in the face of budget cuts as you can demonstrate the clear link between inputs and outputs and therefore the logical consequence of reducing the resources made available to you.

Here's a list of some other Dos and Don'ts.
Don't pad your budget to give yourself an easy life. Budgeting is about allocating scarce resources in the optimum way to maximise the long-

term financial performance of the business. So don't hog resources that could have been used profitably elsewhere.

Do be clear about the assumptions you have made. This will allow those reviewing your budget to make sure these are consistent throughout the business (e.g. if you've budgeted to invest in new equipment, someone needs to budget for the maintenance costs, additional supplies etc.) and will help you later in explaining your under or overspends.

Don't underestimate the importance of the task. Caught in the hurly burly of day-to-day affairs, looking so far ahead may seem an inappropriate use of your time. It isn't. If the business is to move ahead in a co-ordinated and controlled manner there needs to be a clearly-communicated plan to avoid people working frantically but, because they're unwittingly pulling against each other, getting nowhere.

Do involve those around you. The more people involved in drawing up the plans, the greater the commitment.

Don't make it an annual event. Keep a budget log (see below) and keep looking 12 months ahead. It's easier to keep adjusting the plan rather than starting with a piece of blank paper once a year however …

Don't do a 'last year plus inflation' budget. The budget is about the future not the past. An understanding of the costs you've incurred this year can help you plan for the future but the one thing you know for certain about next year is that it will be different.

Don't leave it to accountants!

And even when that budget has been agreed and signed off...

Don't file it away because you now have the task of …

Controlling the numbers

Your budget sets out the resources that have been agreed you need to fulfil your part of the team plan. Resources are limited so it's important you use the ones made available to you as effectively as possible.

A budget is not a licence to spend! If you can achieve the tasks required of you with fewer resources than you thought you'd need, all the better. That creates the opportunity for the business to go ahead with other proposals that had previously been deferred for want of adequate resources.

The more thought you put into your planning and budgeting, the easier it will be to monitor how you're doing and understand reported savings and overspends. These reports should not throw up any surprises if you're in control of what you're doing and keep an eye on the plan. You should know whether a task is taking more or less time than forecast; you know at the point of authorisation whether an item of expenditure is more expensive or cheaper than planned.

Only costs for which you are responsible and can control should be on your budget. The accountant may apportion costs across the business for other reasons (e.g. costing) but that should not happen for the purpose of budgetary control.

As you go along, keep a diary or budget log in which you note down significant abnormal activities or unexpected 'one-off' costs. This will help you understand your costs and therefore improve the quality of your forecasting.

Inevitably all will not go exactly to plan. So you have to act. There's no point having a plan and monitoring your progress against that plan if it doesn't result in any actions. Firstly check whether the saving or overspend is just a matter of timing. If so, make sure that those co-ordinating the financial results understand this. Where there are deliverable savings flag up the opportunity to use those resources elsewhere. Don't assume you have the 'right' to use them to cross-subsidise an overspend on one of your other budgets or on a 'pet project'. Where there is an irretrievable overspend this needs drawing to the attention of the accountant who will need to make revisions to their forecast.

Budgets are set to optimally allocate scarce resources at a point in time and needs change. It's helpful if you have the type of business culture where budget-holders get together on a regular basis to update each other on how they're doing so that resources can be re-allocated if necessary in the best-interests of the business. If for instance energy prices rise faster than anticipated and the site manager is faced with an unavoidable major overspend, there may be actions others can take to alleviate the situation. The sales manager may decide they could delay the appointment of a new administrator for a month thereby saving salary costs. The maintenance manager may postpone the plan to bring in decorators to re-paint the canteen. And the human resources manager could immediately launch an energy-saving initiative.

7. COSTING

INTRODUCTION

You're in business to make money.

To do this you need to be selling your products or services for more than they cost.

How do you know if you're doing this? You have invoices that tell you how much your customer values what you are doing – but what about your costs?

All businesses do this:

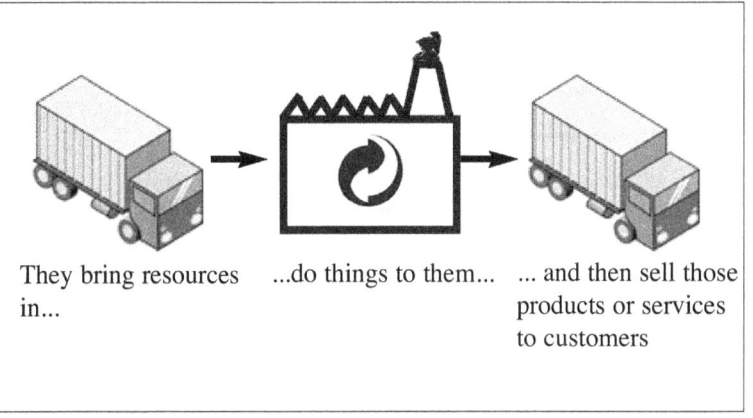

They bring resources in... ...do things to them... ... and then sell those products or services to customers

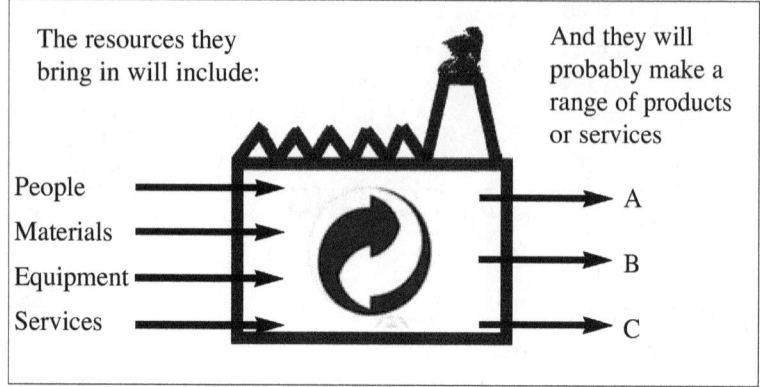

But which resources were required to make each product or service?

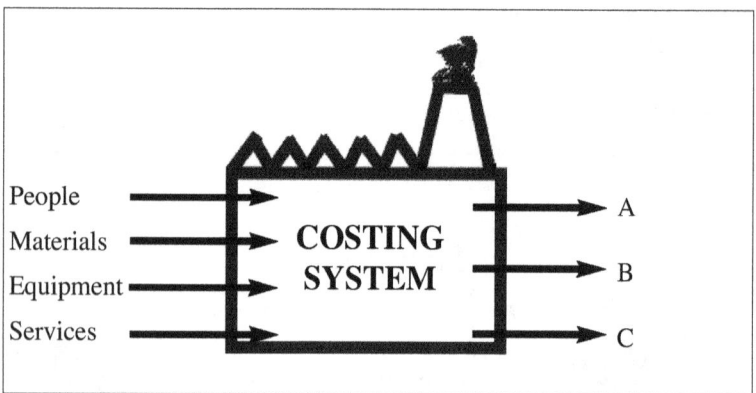

The logic-link put in place to match resources to outputs is the costing system.

UNDERSTANDING YOUR COSTS IS CRITICAL TO UNDERSTANDING YOUR BUSINESS

You use costing information to determine product margins and therefore whether individual products or services are 'good' or 'bad' for business. This drives marketing decisions such as encouraging your sales team to identify more market opportunities for profitable lines whilst cutting 'loss-makers' from your portfolio

If you're looking for ways to improve your profits by driving down your costs you need to understand where those costs are being incurred and be able to measure whether your actions have had the desired effect.

You also want to be able to weigh-up the costs of operational choices available to you; for example, do you continue to do a task in-house or do you outsource?

Where do you look for the information for these types of decisions?

All too often it is assumed that it is readily available and can be lifted directly from the costing system. After all, when you report your product or service costs so accurately (often to several decimal places) they must be correct... mustn't they?

The harsh reality is that cost information is a matter of professional judgement. Give 12 highly qualified accountants the task of costing one of your products or services through the business and they will come up with 12 different correct answers. All of these answers would pass the audit test. Not only would the 12 answers differ, but also it is highly probable that none of them would be relevant in assisting you with the decision you are trying to take.

It is therefore important that you understand the basis of any cost information provided and can adjust it, where appropriate, to suit the purpose for which you intend to use it.

It is worth noting that one of the things you rarely use your costing information for is pricing. Few businesses are able to price their products or services on a 'cost-plus' basis. The market sets the price based on the value it places on your offering. Having therefore made sure that your customers maximise their perception of the value offered (not just of the more obvious product or service attributes but also your excellent quality, reliable on-time delivery etc.) you then price at the highest level you can and still win the business.

But not any business

You do need to have an understanding of your costs to know when to walk away from the table and decline to bid – or, for strategic reasons, take on unprofitable work while understanding the financial impact it will have on your business.

REPORTING COSTS
External reporting
External reporting requires the compilation of "attributable cost" to measure against the value of sales in determining profit in the Profit & Loss Account (see p.38).

The difference between the total costs the business has incurred and those that have 'left' the business through the Profit and Loss Account will be the value of inventory that is shown on the Balance Sheet.

As external reports require stock to be valued at the total cost incurred in bringing it to its current condition (i.e. as raw material, WIP or finished goods) both the Profit and Loss figure for attributable cost and the Balance Sheet value of inventory are usually calculated using an "overhead absorption costing" system. In such systems product or service costs include material and labour together with overhead costs such as supervisory salaries, electricity, depreciation and rent that are 'loaded' on to those product or service costs through the use of cost rates (see below).

[In businesses with internal costing systems where products or services costs just include the costs of material and labour, rather than having to introduce a second parallel costing system, if the overhead element of the inventory value is relatively small or can be confidently estimated, auditors may be satisfied with a reasoned uplift to be added to the internal cost to allow for the overhead.]

In financial reports, costs should be at 'actual' so if your business uses a standard costing system (see Appendix 8) an adjustment will have to be made to bring those standard, or predicted, costs back to actuals.

Internal Reporting
Whereas there are rules for the compilation of costing information for external reporting, no such rules apply for internal reports. The purpose of internal reporting is to provide colleagues with useful information to help inform them in their decision-making. Some businesses will use the same approach for both external and internal reporting. Others will choose to 'cut and dice' the data in a different way.

The job of the costing system is to mirror the reality of what is going on in the business by reflecting the resources required to make each product or deliver each service. Look back at that diagram on p.82.

There are no two businesses that bring in identical resources and do exactly the same things to them in exactly the same way so as to produce exactly the same products. Therefore no two businesses should have identical costing systems.

But there are common approaches used some of which are explained in the next section.

COSTING TECHNIQUES

Look back at the diagram on p.82 showing the costing system as the logic-link between the resources brought into the business (i.e. the costs incurred) and the products or services that you are in business to make.

The logic-link you choose will determine which of those resources are deemed to have 'gone out of the business on the back of a lorry to the customer' (i.e. have been sold) and the ones that remain in the business as inventory. The technique chosen will also determine the way in which cost information is reported.

Take a look at some of the different kinds of resources coming into the business:

- Direct Materials
- Direct Labour
- Production Overheads
  e.g. production supervisors' and managers' salaries, utilities, depreciation of equipment, rent and rates
- Other Costs (often referred to as SG&A – Sales and General Admin)
  e.g. sales department salaries and expenses, administration salaries and expenses

Direct materials are those that form an integral part of the products or services you are producing. For example, the flour you use in the bread you sell would be a direct material whereas the material you use to clean your ovens would not.

Direct labour are the payroll costs of the people who are seen to work on the product or perform the service rather than those carrying out supervisory or administrative functions.

Production overheads are those payroll and other costs incurred in supporting the manufacture of the product or the delivery of the service other than direct materials and direct labour.

A word of warning. This is an area fraught with localised terminology and the use of generic jargon used in unique ways. Take the wrapper off terms used in your business such as "indirect costs", "overheads" and "expenses"; then look at what's inside and you'll see where they fit in the spectrum.

As you go down the above list you can see that it becomes increasingly difficult to find an accurate way of attributing resources to products or services.

Direct materials are relatively easy to attribute. After all, you can either purchase materials specifically for a product or a contract and collect the costs this way (an approach known as "job costing") or you can have a list of the materials you need for each product or service you supply (often referred to as a "bill of materials" or BOM) and use this to cost the materials used.

Nor is direct labour too hard to deal with. You can either have people booking to a specific product or contract (job costing) or have a list of the tasks that have to be carried out to complete a product or deliver a service (often referred to in manufacturing as a "layout") and use this to cost the labour you have used.

Beyond this it gets difficult:

- How do you determine how much supervisory time was required for contract A rather than contract B?
- What about the relative cost of electricity they required?
- How much depreciation should each contract bear?
- What about rent and rates?
- How do you determine the cost of the administration support they required? What about the selling costs?

If your business wants to include these kinds of costs into the reported costs of products or services they're going to have to use some form of absorption costing whereby products or services absorb these 'non-direct' costs through the application of cost rates.

These rates are also known appropriately as burden rates as costs are 'loaded' on to the back of products or services travelling through the business on their way out to a customer.

Absorption Costing

Advocates of full absorption costing are of the opinion that all business costs (other than financing) should be attributed to the cost of products or services you supply and therefore include them all in the costing system. Those referring to their costing systems as being of the overhead absorption variety usually exclude the resources used outside production activities (i.e. those used in support activities such as selling and administration) from the costing system and write these costs off as and when they are incurred.

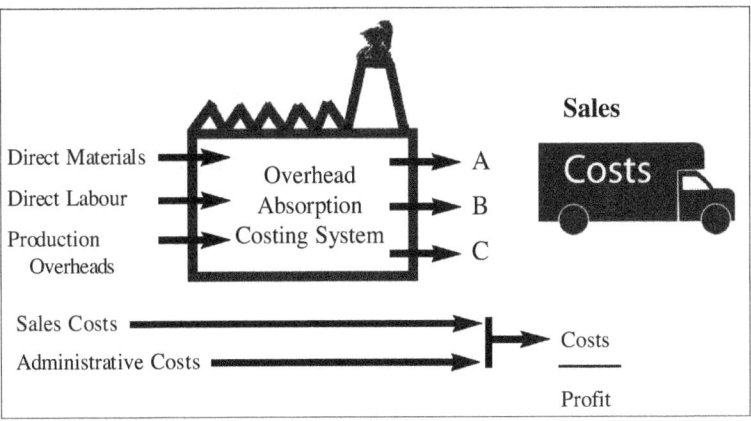

This means they are entered straight into the Profit and Loss Account as a cost of doing business in that period.

If you've ever heard accountants talk about whether a cost is "above the line" or "below the line" they'll be discussing whether it should form part of the product or service cost (i.e. be "above" and go into the costing system) or be simply written off as and when incurred (i.e. be "below" the line).

For the sake of simplicity the term overhead will be used from this point onwards to describe any 'non-direct' cost that is to be included in the costing system. Whatever the range of costs included in these overheads, you'll need some basis for absorbing them into your product or service costs.

The first step is to decide what will be your cost centres (sometimes referred to as cells). These cost centres will provide particular processes (e.g. one might do machining, another assembly) through which your products or services may pass on their way out to the customer. Not all products or services will necessarily travel through the same cost centres, neither will they necessarily place the same demands upon them.

For example, product X might need to pass through a machining, plating and assembly process; product Y just requires machining and assembly; product Z may just require assembly.

Once these cost centres have been decided, the next step is to determine the overhead costs that 'belong' to each cost centre through a process of allocation and apportionment. For example if supervisors work in specific cost centres, their payroll costs can be allocated specifically to that centre.

Not all costs are so easily allocated, however. What about your electricity bill? Unless you resort to having a meter fitted to each cost centre area you're going to have to apportion overheads on some appropriate basis. If most of the electricity costs go on heating, you might want to do this on the basis of floor area. If, however, the key determinant is the power used by machines, you may decide that an apportionment based on the horsepower of machines in each cost centre is more appropriate.

Once you've gone through all your overheads allocating and apportioning you will now have a total overhead cost for each cost centre.

You still have to find some way of passing the cost of running each cost centre on to the back of those products or services that require its capability and this is done through applying a cost rate.

By looking at the forecast you can determine the demand for each cost centre's services. You can then use this as shown below to calculate the cost rate at which overheads should be charged. Some businesses include the direct labour cost in with the overhead therefore coming up with a "labour and overhead" rate.

For example, if the result of allocating and apportioning the overhead costs shows a total overhead cost to run a cost centre of £200,000 and the forecast shows that 2,000 hours of work are scheduled to take place in that centre, the cost rate will be:

$$\frac{£200,000}{2,000 \text{ hours}} = £100 \text{ per hour}$$

For each hour of work a product or service requires in this cost centre, it will 'pick up' £100 of overhead costs.

If all goes according to plan and the overheads actually cost £200,000 and 2,000 hours of work are actually carried out, then the objective will have been met with all the overheads passed out on to the backs of products. Of course, things won't go exactly to plan and inevitably you will "under" or "over" absorb your overheads.

You "under absorb" (bad news) if you spend more than you expected and/or fail to generate 2,000 hours of work – i.e. your actual cost rate is higher than planned.

You "over absorb" (good news) if you spend less than expected and/or generate more than 2,000 hours of work – i.e. your actual cost rate is lower than that set.

In a business where there is a significant cost in managing the supply chain, one of the cost centres may be the cost of sourcing, purchasing and receiving materials. Having reached a total cost for the centre (as part of the allocation and apportionment process referred to above) this cost is usually absorbed on the basis of the value of materials purchased.

For example, if the supply chain cost is £100,000 and £1,000,000 of materials are forecast to be purchased in the year, the cost rate will be:

$$\frac{£100,000}{£1,000,000} = 10\%$$

Every material purchase will be 'marked up' by 10% to cover the overheads. This mark-up is often referred to as a handling rate.

Businesses using an overhead absorption costing system would report in a format along these lines:

	Product X	**Product Y**	**Total**
	£	£	£
Sales	800,000	200,000	1,000,000
Direct Mats.	30,000	70,000	100,000
Direct Lab.	180,000	20,000	200,000
Production Overheads	360,000	40,000	400,000
Cost of Sales	570,000	130,000	700,000
Gross Profit	230,000	70,000	300,000
Selling			85,000
Admin.			115,000
Operating Profit			£100,000

Activity Based Costing (ABC)

ABC is another form of absorption costing (usually a "full" one, including all the costs) but it approaches the establishment of cost centres from a different perspective.

Here it is argued that people do not manage costs, they manage activities that cause cost to be incurred e.g. taking orders from customers, purchasing materials, setting-up machines, running machines, packaging and delivering products. Therefore the higher the demand a product or service places on those activities, the higher should be the cost.

The first step is to identify the activities that are going to be used as cost centres.

The next step is to decide on the "key drivers" (the factors responsible for determining the level of demand placed on each activity.)

The "activity cost rates" are then calculated by taking the cost of the activity and dividing it by the number of times that activity is expected to be demanded in a year.

Take the example of a business that decides that one of its main activities is that of sourcing, progressing and receiving parts into the business and that products requiring lots of components should therefore pick up more of these costs than those that don't. If the costs incurred in supporting those activities bringing parts into the business is £150,000 and the number of parts brought in during the year is expected to be 7,500 then products would pick up £20 cost for every part they require.

If, instead, the number of purchase orders placed is seen to be the key driver, and it is expected that 3,000 orders will be raised, products would pick up a cost of £50 for every purchase order issued for them.

Contribution Costing

This approach sorts the costs into "variable" (those that will increase or decrease with the volume of activity) and "fixed" costs (those that will not). Variable costs would include costs such as materials, whereas rent and rates would be treated as fixed. The variable costs would go into the costing system whereas the fixed costs would not.

The difference between the selling price of an item and its variable cost is referred to as its contribution and is the amount that it can contribute to 'the pot'. The money in the pot must firstly cover the fixed costs. At the point at which this happens, the business "breaks even". The contribution from every unit sold beyond this point will therefore form the period's profit.

	Product X	**Product Y**	**Total**
	£	£	£
Sales	800,000	200,000	1,000,000
Less Variable Costs	243,750	93,750	337,500
Contribution	556,250	106,250	662,500
Fixed Costs			562,500
Operating Profit			£100,000

Lean Accounting

Lean Accounting is not about having an efficient accounting system that produces accounting information in a waste-free timely manner (although that's an aspect of "lean" that should be looked at). It is about producing relevant information to steer the business on its improvement journey – and that includes the way products and services are costed.

Any form of allocation is an anathema to the lean protagonist who would regard virtually everyone in the organisation as direct to one of the "valuestreams" (usually product or product types) running through the business – and, if this were not the case, would want to reorganise the organisational structure so that they were. The same view would be taken for virtually all other costs.

With the exception of materials, costs are seen to be the result of having taken the decision to offer that valuestream's capability to the market and therefore should be written off in the month in which they are incurred. Inventory is therefore valued at material cost only.

	Valuestream A £	Valuestream B £	Total £
Sales	800,000	200,000	1,000,000
Cost of materials used	30,000	70,000	100,000
Valuestream Costs	580,000	100,000	680,000
Valuestream Profit	190,000	30,000	220,000
Business Costs			120,000
Operating Profit			100,000

MASTERING COSTING INFORMATION
A Cautionary Note

Changing your costing system doesn't change the underlying financial performance of your business.

It may cause a 'blip' in the profit figure and your stock valuation if you rethink which costs are going to be written-off to the Profit and Loss Account and those that you will store away on the Balance Sheet until those products or services to which they've been attributed are eventually sold. But when it comes to the crunch you haven't fundamentally changed a thing. You've bought the same things for the same amount of money and sold the same things at the same prices. If you want to make more money you need to increase sales and/or reduce costs, not just reshuffle them. It's not about how you cut the cake – it is about the size of the cake you're cutting.

To master the numbers you need to critically assess the costing information available to you.

Set aside those external reports. You don't manage your business from them. Turn to the management reports. Look at the cost of your products or services and then drill down to ascertain how those costs have been compiled. Remember that your costing system is the slave not the master. Its job is to reflect what is happening in your business.

Is the information provided useful – or even remotely relevant – to the decisions you are taking?

Costing Systems Compared
Absorption systems

These systems are criticised for being not just useless, but positively misleading for most decision-making. Yet the costing information they provide may look impressively accurate. But look at where those costs came from and the 'professional judgements' that went into their compilation.

- Which costs are to be included in the system and which are to be treated as 'below-the-line'?
- How many cost centres should there be?
- How should the boundaries between cost centres be drawn?
- What data collection systems should be put in place so that costs can be allocated rather than apportioned?
- Where costs are apportioned on what basis should this be done?
- What should be used as the denominator (the item at the bottom) in calculating the cost rate – e.g. labour hours or machine hours?

The choices made determine the costing information provided.
Change the choices and the product costs change.
So don't be deceived by those decimal places. Whatever costing system you use it should 'mirror the reality' of what is going on in the business.

Absorption costing systems were used in manufacturing businesses at the start of the 20th century. Picture the reality of a factory at that time. A building stuffed with people 'turning the handle on machines'. With such a high proportion of direct costs (people and materials) any weakness in the way other costs were absorbed was unlikely to be significant.

Contrast that with businesses today. Take a look at the spectrum of your costs and determine what those proportions are now. The greater the proportion of costs to be absorbed the increased likelihood of a distorted reflection from that mirror.

But the main attack on absorption costing comes from those who cite its irrelevance to decision-making and the way it can encourage 'bad behaviour'. For instance, you want to hold the minimum amount of inventory you can whilst meeting the needs of your customers (see p.31 if you're unsure why this is).

You also get what you measure. An over-fixation on cost rates will motivate people to make sure they get 'the hours' regardless of whether customers want those jobs or not. Whilst this lowers the cost rate and therefore makes the products you do sell look cheaper, all you have really done is to hide costs away in your Balance Sheet under the disguise of unnecessary inventory.

Example:

- Customers have placed orders for 2,000 units of product;
- Each unit requires £90 material and 1 hour of work;
- Labour is paid at £10 per hour;
- Overhead costs are £200,000.

If just the 2,000 hours of work necessary to fulfil the customers' orders are done the overhead rate is:

$$\frac{£200,000}{2,000 \text{ hours}} = £100 \text{ per hour}$$

The unit product cost would therefore be:

	£
Direct Material	90
Direct Labour	10
Production Overhead	100
Product Cost	200

and there would be no inventory.

If the selling price were £250 the profit per unit would be £50.

If, however, the decision were taken to work 2,500 hours and therefore make 2,500 items the overhead rate would be:

$$\frac{£200,000}{2,500 \text{ hours}} = £80 \text{ per hour}$$

The unit product cost would therefore be:

	£
Direct Material	90
Direct Labour	10
Production Overhead	80
Product Cost	180

With a selling price of £250 the profit per unit has jumped to £70.

But is the product really more profitable?
There would now be 500 units in inventory at a value of £90,000; i.e. The business has spent £45,000 on materials (500 units x £90) and paid their workforce £5,000 (500 units x £10) to carry out work they didn't need. Add to this the £40,000 of overhead cost they've already incurred but have 'hidden away' by attaching it to items that have not yet been sold, and you have the £90,000 of inventory. What a farce!

When it comes to using costing information for decision-making get ready to 'strip down' and 'reassemble' those costs. Think about which of the costs going into those rates are relevant to the decision.

Have you ever walked through a factory and seen a state-of-the-art piece of equipment standing idle whilst an antiquated relic is crunching its way through the job? The reason? The cost rate given for using the new machine is very high and it is therefore calculated to be 'cheaper', even though it takes longer, to use the old equipment.

What a nonsense. The rate for the new equipment would include a meaty chunk of depreciation – a 'sunk' cost, one that has 'been and gone' and is therefore irrelevant in deciding which machine to use.

What about the make/buy decision? Setting aside considerations other than the purely financial (such as whether you would be in danger of setting up a future competitor or one who could cut you out and deliver direct to your customer), would it be cheaper to carry out this work at a sub-contractor rather than do it yourself?

Don't use an unadulterated absorption cost-rate for the cost comparison! Go through your costs and identify what incremental savings or additional costs you would incur if you did outsource. Unless in so-doing you can bring in other work you had previously outsourced or relieve a bottleneck in your operation that is constraining the amount you can pull through your business for your customers, you are likely to end up paying your suppliers' overheads as well as your own!

The same problem arises with quantifying the financial benefit from "improvement" activities. Assume your cost rate is £50 per hour. If you save an hour in the time it takes to make a product you won't make a cost-saving of £50 – unless you can fill that hour with productive work you would otherwise have been unable to do. After all, virtually all those costs included in the rate will still be there.

Activity Based Costing

The introduction of the ABC approach was not a panacea for all known illnesses but it did the trick of opening people's minds to the fact that there was not just one way, the traditional absorption method, to cost products. Two of the criticisms of absorption costing were that it usually failed to encompass all the business costs (therefore giving a usually false impression that somehow all those other below-the-line costs would fall proportionately across the product range) and that the way cost rates were calculated meant they failed to pick up on where one product caused 'more hassle' than another – and where there's hassle there's cost.

By covering all costs and using activities as the basis for cost rates, ABC is an interesting approach. Many criticise it as being expensive to set up and maintain and of little relevance to decision-making.

It does however have its uses. Done as an occasional rough exercise it can provide a 'health-check' on your costing system to see whether the information you're currently being provided with is substantially skewed and therefore at danger of pointing you in the wrong direction (see Appendix 9, Product Life-Cycles).

It can also help to assess the impact on costs of a proposed change in product mix by highlighting activities for which there will be increased or decreased levels of demand.

And it can trigger cost improvement activities. If, for example, the activity rates calculated show a cost of £100 to raise a purchase order, two things should happen. First there will be an attempt to reduce the number of purchase orders placed to 'avoid' the cost (of course there is no real saving to the business until the costs that go into the calculation of the activity rate are reduced as a result of the reduction in demand for the activity) and second there will be an enthusiasm to re-engineer the process to make the activity of raising a purchase order cheaper.

Contribution Costing

The obvious difficulty here is deciding which costs are variable and which are fixed for the timescale under consideration. Direct labour costs are a particularly tricky one. There will be other costs that are semi-variable, e.g. electricity and delivery vehicle costs. Therefore, it is important to know where the line has been drawn so that you can make any necessary adjustments if using this information as a starting-point for your decisions.

It could be argued that this is very useful information for some decision-making. If you know the variable (or "marginal") cost of a product or service, you know that if you can sell it at a price in excess of that cost the difference will make a positive contribution to the business' bottom line.

But that information can also be extremely dangerous in the wrong hands! Just selling products or services at a price above their variable costs isn't sufficient. Making a contribution may be enough for that incremental opportunity whereby pricing competitively (whilst not upsetting your existing customer base) you can fill short-term surplus capacity by winning an order that you might otherwise have lost; but, as a rule, you need to be taking on business that covers your fixed costs and provides sufficient profit to make the business a worthwhile venture.

(Not only that, but don't forget to think through the implications of any additional investment required on the Balance Sheet. The increased investment required in *Working Capital* when taking on additional business is often overlooked. Remember that it's not profit you're after but *profitability* – see p.62.)

If you can't sell at a price that covers all your costs and earns enough profit to make the business sustainable into the future then there's something wrong with how you've aligned your business to the market.

Perhaps full absorption costing, taken with a pinch of salt, has a role to play after all!

Lean Accounting

With all costs other than material being written-off as incurred, the internal Profit and Loss Account gives a clear statement of the financial cost of providing the capability offered to the market as a valuestream and whether the market has taken up that offering.

If the business is correctly aligned it will have been able to pull orders for the customer through the business at a price that has allowed it to recoup those costs.

There is clarity of vision here. To improve profit the business must attract more orders and/or have customers value their offering more highly and/or organise their valuestream more efficiently by eliminating waste. With no cost absorption to lead you down the wrong track, decision-making is guided by looking at the incremental financial costs and benefits to the valuestream.

8. CAPITAL EXPENDITURE APPRAISAL (CAPEX)

INTRODUCTION

Your heart sinks. You want to buy some new equipment and you've just been told that, as it is categorised as Capital Expenditure, you'll have to submit a CAPEX request. The convoluted time-consuming processes these applications go through are legendary – why is it so difficult to get approval for such expenditure?

Of course the amount of money involved is often relatively substantial for the business and therefore a significant financial commitment. But it's more than this.

Capital expenditure (the purchase of *fixed assets*) is a strategic decision. By definition it involves the purchase of an asset that will, it has been argued, bring 'value' to the business for a number of years. Your fixed assets define the capability you offer in the marketplace. When you carry out capital expenditure you lay out the way you're intending to meet market needs for many years into the future. If you get this strategic choice wrong and your competitors get it right it can kill your business.

Who do you want to pay for your capital expenditure? Ultimately, your customers. The selling price for your goods or services is almost always determined by the marketplace, not by how much it has cost you to meet those needs. So if you get the capital expenditure decision right, the market places a value on your products or services that exceeds your costs. All your costs, including the cost of the investment you've made in those fixed assets. Customers however will not pay you a premium to compensate you if you've chosen a process that is not as cost-efficient as your competitors.

Before evaluating the financials there will need to be a discussion about the strategic implications of the proposed investment to make sure it fits with the direction the business is taking. Once that has been agreed then it's time to start work on the numbers.

[*Note:* Before launching into the CAPEX process do check you need to do this. Businesses need to be pragmatic. Whilst in theory any investment that is made that will result in an asset that is of use to the business over a number of years is a fixed asset, and therefore constitutes capital expenditure, businesses will have a threshold beneath which small value purchases are treated as part of the normal running costs – i.e. "revenue" rather than "capital". This threshold will be determined by the size of the business and the emphasis placed on scrutinising proposed expenditure.]

SETTING OUT THE CASE

Don't start with the numbers, start with the story.

Why does the investment seem an attractive proposition?

Make a list of all the impacts (positive and negative) of the proposed project. The financial evaluation will be based on the "incremental" cash inflows and outflows that would result from the investment so, when drawing up this list, keep asking yourself, "What difference would this project make to the business?"

Here are some thoughts to get you started.
If the focus of your proposal is to increase sales:

- Will there be an increase in the volume of existing products or additional lines?
- Perhaps you're proposing to increase prices (or reduce warranty costs) as a result of improved quality?
- What additional equipment would you need?
- Would you need to increase the workforce who make the product or deliver the service?
- Will you need additional materials?
- Would you need to increase your salesforce and/or your marketing activities?

- What impact will it have on your packaging and distribution costs?

If the focus is around cost-saving:

- What would you need to buy?
- Where would you expect savings to be made?
- Will you need as many people, or as much overtime?
- Perhaps you won't have to use as much material or could save on the space the business occupies?

This is why CAPEX submissions should not be left to accountants!

You are the one best-placed to articulate what your proposal would involve and what it would offer. By all means run your list past colleagues to see if they can spot anything you've missed.

The next step is to quantify those incremental impacts
For example:

- "We will sell an additional 100 units of product per month."
- "We will save 20 hours of overtime each week."
  (Note the absence of £ notes at this stage!)

This is the hardest step of all in the CAPEX process.

"You can't make a silk purse out of a sow's ear."

It's a classic case of GIGO – "Garbage In Garbage Out". All the fancy financial evaluation techniques in the world can't make a sensible decision from incorrect information.

Take each item on your list in turn. Talk to those who might be able to help. Given that the nature of the investment is to spend money now to get benefits in the future there will inevitably be some uncertainty.

Allow for the personalities of those involved – some colleagues will be born optimists others cautious pessimists. Especially where the impact is significant to the decision, ask people for their 'best case' and 'worst case' scenarios as this will help you later when you're doing *sensitivity analyses*. It might help you improve the quality of the information you're given if you also remind people that the post-audit phase will provide everyone with the opportunity to re-visit their forecasts and reflect on the accuracy of the predictions they made as part of a feedback and learning process.

The final step is to express those quantified impacts in financial terms – so a helpful accountant at this stage can be invaluable!

Here's a simple example:

The designer has spent the last 6 months (and £90,000) creating a new product for the range.
The sales manager wants to make the case for bringing it to market so collects the following information:

– A pre-launch marketing campaign would be required costing £50,000 with additional advertising costs of £10,000 per annum.
– The market life for this product is expected to be 3 years with sales volumes and prices as follows:

	Units	**Price(£/Unit)**
Year 1	1,000	200
Year 2	2,000	180
Year 3	1,250	160

– If given approval to proceed, the company would have to buy a dedicated machine which will cost £200,000.
– The company depreciates machines over 5 years.
– The cost/unit for materials and labour is projected to be:

	Cost(£/Unit)
Year 1	110
Year 2	100
Year 3	80

– Overheads are allocated to products at 100% materials and labour

The first step is to produce a table identifying the incremental cash flows with the outflows shown in brackets.

Year	0 (Now)	1	2	3
	£	£	£	£
Design Cost	(50,000)			
Marketing				
Advertising		(10,000)	(10,000)	(10,000)
New Machine	(200,000)			
Sales Revenue		200,000	360,000	200,000
Mat/Lab Costs		(110,000)	(200,000)	(100,000)
Depreciation				
Overheads				
Cash flow	**(250,000)**	**80,000**	**150,000**	**90,000**

Note that some of the information gathered does not result in any incremental cash flows:

- Design cost – this is a "sunk cost". It has already happened; whether the project proceeds or not will make no difference so it is therefore not an 'incremental' cash flow.
- Depreciation – there is no cash flowing when depreciation is charged. The cost of buying the equipment is included as a cash outflow at the time of purchase.
- Overheads – all the incremental costs have already been included elsewhere so the accountant's allocation of existing cost is not relevant.

[*A word of warning.* When carrying out your own project appraisal, remember you are just looking for incremental cash flows. Be extremely wary of how you use any 'cost' information provided to you for this purpose. In all probability, using cost information such as cost rates lifted straight from your costing system will not give you the right answer as they will include costs that will not change regardless of whether you go ahead with your project or not – e.g. rent and rates (see Chapter 7 – Costing)]

It is important to emphasise that the evaluation techniques that follow just use the figures from that bottom line of the table, the total projected cash flows in each year. They evaluate whether it is worth proceeding with a project that would require spending £250,000 now for predicted cash inflows of £80,000 in Year 1; £150,000 in Year 2; and £90,000 in Year 3.

Note what these numbers really are – the summation of 'best estimates'. Remember the numbers generated by these techniques will only be as good as the information that was provided.

THE FINANCIAL EVALUATION

There are a number of evaluation techniques that you (or your accountant) may carry out on your proposal.

Payback

This is the simplest technique and identifies the time it would take for the project to recoup the initial outlay if all goes according to plan.

The cumulative cash inflows are calculated so that the point at which the project is forecast to recover the initial outlay can be determined.

The shorter the payback period, the more attractive the project.

Using the example from p.103:

	Net Cash Flow (NCF) £	**Cumulative Net Cash Flow** (Cum. NCF) £	
Year 1	80,000	80,000	
Year 2	150,000	230,000	
Year 3	90,000	320,000	← Payback

Initial Investment: £250,000

The initial outlay should be recouped in just over 2 years.

If a greater level of accuracy is required this may be done by interpolation. By the end of year 2 a further £20,000 is needed to payback the £250,000. As £90,000 is expected to flow in during year 3 the payback point would be calculated as:

Payback = 2 yrs + (£20,000/£90,000) yrs = 2.2 yrs (or 2yrs 3mths)

One of the strengths of the technique is that it is straightforward and easy to understand and interpret. Another strength is its focus on the early years. Projects involving CAPEX extend into the future often over many years. Wherever there are forecasts there is uncertainty. It is reasonable to assume the short-term is easier to predict than the long-term; so, in this respect, the shorter the payback period, the lower the risk.

But this focus on the short-term, just to the point of payback, is also the technique's major weakness.

Consider these three projects:

Project	A	B	C
	£	£	£
Initial Outlay	10,000	10,000	10,000
Net Cash Flow:			
Year 1	10,000	2,000	2,000
Year 2	–	8,000	4,000
Year 3	–	2,000	6,000
Year 4	–	1,000	8,000
Year 5	–	1,000	10,000
Payback:	1 year	2 years	2.7 years

If you select on payback period alone, you'll choose A. Aren't you tempted by B or C even if you do have to wait a little longer to recover your initial outlay? It's therefore useful to do payback alongside one of the other methods that takes into consideration all the project cash flows.

[*Note:* Payback periods and depreciation periods are not the same thing. The payback period is the time it takes to recover your initial project outlay and is part of the CAPEX decision. If the project is approved any fixed assets purchased will then be depreciated over their useful life to the business to enable profit figures to be meaningful – see Appendix 3, Fixed Assets.]

Discounted Cash Flows (DCF)

Another of the weaknesses of the simple payback calculation is that it fails to consider the 'time' value of money.

Assume interest rates are 10%. If you were given £1,000 you could invest it in the bank and at the end of a year you would have £1,100.

So if you invest £1,000 in a project that will pay back £1,000 in a year's time is that good enough?

No. You'd want to get back at least £1,100 as that is what you could have earned just putting your money in the bank. Cash received in the future is therefore not as valuable to you as cash received today.

In DCF techniques, discount factors are applied to "discount" future cash inflows to 'today's money terms' allowing a more meaningful comparison of the relative worth of cash flows over a period of time. [For an explanation of the calculation and interpretation of discount factors see Appendix 7, Discounted Cash Flows.]

The DCF techniques most commonly used are explained below.

Net Present Value (NPV)

The NPV of the project is the value to the business, in today's money terms, of proceeding with the project. The higher the NPV the more attractive the project.

The first step is to establish the discount rate the business uses. (This will reflect the average cost of the capital available to them.)

Discount tables are then used to identify the discount factors to be applied to each of the annual cash flows to determine their NPV. The total of these NPVs can then be compared with the initial outlay to determine whether the project is 'worth doing'.

If the overall NPV is positive the project is acceptable on this criterion; if it is negative it is not.

Using the example on p.103 and assuming a discount rate of 10%:

	NCF £	Discount Factor 10%	NPV £
Year 1	80,000	0.909	72,720
Year 2	150,000	0.826	123,900
Year 3	90,000	0.751	67,590
			264,210
		Initial Investment:	250,000
		Project NPV:	14,210

In this case the overall NPV is positive making the project acceptable on this basis – the business will be £14,210 'better off' if it proceeds with the project.

It's interesting that at this point people invariably get twitchy and note that "it's a bit close, isn't it?" Of course, ultimately, whether the business wins or loses from going ahead with the project will depend on the accuracy of the forecast.

The advantages of using NPV are that it allows for the time value of money and considers all the cash flows throughout the lifetime of the project.

The disadvantages are that there will inevitably be some question over the appropriate discount rate to use and that a simplistic approach of 'the highest NPV wins' gives no consideration of the differing scales of competing projects, as shown in the example below.

Project Alpha requires an initial outlay of £3,000 whereas Project Beta requires £30,000. The project cash flows (NCF) for the 4 year life of the projects are included in the table below:

	Discount Factor (10%)	**ALPHA**		**BETA**	
		NCF (£)	**NPV (£)**	**NCF (£)**	**NPV(£)**
Year 1	0.909	1,000	909	10,000	9,090
Year 2	0.826	1,000	826	10,000	8,260
Year 3	0.751	1,000	751	10,000	7,510
Year 4	0.683	1,000	683	10,000	6,830
			3,169		31,690
Initial Investment:			3,000		30,000
Project NPV:			169		1,690

Discounted Payback
Some businesses prefer to see the payback calculation (see p.104) carried out on discounted rather than absolute cash flows.

Using the original example and the net present values of the annual flows as shown on p.106:

	NCF	Discount Factor	NPV	Cumulative NPV
	£	10%	£	£
Year 1	80,000	0.909	72,720	72,720
Year 2	150,000	0.826	123,900	196,620
Year 3	90,000	0.751	67,590	264,210 ← Discount Payback

Initial outlay: £250,000

Discounted Payback (using the interpolation method – see p.104):

2 yrs + (£53,380/£67,590) yrs = 2.8 yrs (or 2yrs 9 mths)

Internal Rate of Return (IRR)

Rather than use a specific discount rate, some businesses ask for the project's IRR. This is, in effect, the discount rate at which the project "breaks even" – i.e. where the project NPV would be zero.

As discount rates increase, future cash flows are more aggressively discounted thereby reducing the project NPV.

IRR would usually be determined by using a simple computerised application but it can also be done manually on an iterative basis or by interpolation as shown below.

Using the original example, the project has already been discounted at 10% but is now also discounted at 14%.

	NCF £	Discount Factor 10%	NPV £	Discount Factor 14%	NPV £
Year 1	80,000	0.909	72,720	0.877	70,160
Year 2	150,000	0.826	123,900	0.769	115,350
Year 3	90,000	0.751	67,590	0.675	60,750
			264,210		246,260
		Initial Investment:	250,000		250,000
		Project NPV:	4,210		(3,740)

The IRR, the rate at which the project NPV would be zero, is somewhere between the two rates and can be interpolated to be approximately 13%.

As the IRR is the break-even discount rate for the project, if the business' discount rate rises above the IRR, the future cash inflows no longer compensate for the initial outlay so the project would no longer be financially viable. The IRR therefore helps assess one of the aspects of risk – the amount by which your 'cost of money' would have to change before you would change your mind about the acceptability of the project.

The advantages of this technique are that it allows for the time value of money, it considers all the cash flows, it does not require agreement on a discount rate and can be used when comparing projects of differing scales.

The disadvantages are that the mechanisms of the technique assume that the cash inflows can be re-invested at the same rate as that generated by the underlying project and that, given that there is no consideration of scale, it could encourage the selection of lots of small projects that become difficult to manage.

Most businesses set 'hurdle rates' that projects must meet if they are to be tabled for serious consideration – e.g. the project must payback within 3 years and have an IRR in excess of 12%.

Even if a project passes these tests and is therefore 'acceptable', there will usually be limited cash available and so there will still have to be a competition to decide which projects should go ahead. Such decisions will rest on the contribution the project will make to the strategic plans, the financial returns and, remembering that there is always a weighing-up of risk against return, the relative risks involved.

MASTERING INVESTMENT APPRAISAL

The main problem with capital investment appraisal is that it's about the future. And there's always uncertainty about that. Investments like these usually require the business to 'speculate to accumulate'; to outlay cash now in the expectation of being rewarded with more than compensating cash inflows in the future.

That's a risky business. Whilst any project will carry an element of risk, some are inherently more risky than others – e.g. requiring the use of a technology that is new to the business rather than an extension of existing technology; or launching new products into new markets rather than existing products to new customers. The riskier the project the better the projected returns are going to have to be to make it an attractive proposition.

And speaking of projected returns, look back at that table of incremental cash flows on p.103.

Do you recall that comment about GIGO? The financial techniques that you've just seen only use those 4 figures at the bottom of the table to answer the question:

> "Does it make financial sense to proceed with a project that requires us to spend £250,000 now in return for a cash inflows of £80,000 in the first year then £150,000 in the second year and £90,000 in the third year?"

But where did those numbers come from?
They are the result of adding together a number of 'best guesses'.

How accurate are they going to be?
Hopefully some should be fairly definite – e.g. the cost of buying the machine as quotes should be available.
But what about the incremental sales? How accurate do your sales forecasts tend to be?
What about those incremental cost projections? Do you invariably make the margins you plan to make even on existing business?

Beware the 'spurious accuracy' that can result from throwing a few numbers into financial algorithms that, by their very nature of being merely equations, can appear to 'predict' the outcome very precisely.

There is a balance to be had between risk and return so it's helpful to understand how sensitive your proposal is to the assumptions made in coming up with those cash flows.

You've seen how relatively simple it is to run the numbers through the financial evaluation techniques so take time to run a few different scenarios (often referred to as "what ifs?") to establish how wrong you'd have to be with those best guesses before you would change your mind about whether a project is acceptable or not.

This is also helpful in establishing what are the critical aspects that are key to the success of the project to ensure they are well-managed if the project goes ahead.

When it comes to choosing the financial evaluation techniques to be used it's worth pointing out that it's a good idea for the business to use more than one method. As mentioned earlier, the techniques have strengths and weaknesses so it is helpful to get a more rounded view. Where there are competing projects, the 'rankings' resulting from the evaluations may vary according to the technique used.

Here is a simple example of three competing projects:

	A	B	C
	£k	£k	£k
Initial Outlay	**100**	**100**	**500**
Incremental Cashflows			
Year 1	70	35	0
Year 2	35	35	0
Year 3	15	35	100
Year 4	15	35	300
Year 5	15	35	300
Year 6	15	35	300
	165	210	1,000

Applying the financial techniques already explained the results are as follows:

	A	B	C
Payback	1.9yrs	2.9yrs	4.3yrs
NPV at 10%	£31,833	£52,409	£135,664
IRR	25.7%	26.4%	15.8%

The rankings are therefore:

	1st	2nd	3rd
Payback	A	B	C
NPV at 10%	C	B	A
IRR	B	A	C

No two rankings are the same!

The advantage of using a number of techniques is that you can look for 'trade-offs' – e.g. is it worth waiting an extra year for B to payback compared with A when it brings significantly more value to the business (as measured by the NPV) and has a slightly higher internal rate of return?

If you've done the financial evaluations and you don't like the answers, work out why your project is unattractive. Look back on those predictions you made that resulted in those annual cash flows on which the financial tests were carried out. Review your options.

To improve the result you'll need to:

- reduce outlays
- and/or improve cash inflows
- and/or delay outlays
- and/or expedite inflows.

If the initial outlay includes the purchase of equipment could you:

- Negotiate a better price?
- Negotiate stage payments? – weigh this up carefully if it results in a higher price.
- Lease rather than buy? – again considering any cost and risk implications.

If the benefits on offer are increased sales :

- Have you got the volumes right?
- What about the prices?

- Could you reduce the credit period to customers to get the cash in faster?
- Have you considered stage payments from customers if applicable?

Look at those other costs:

- Have you just included incrementals?
- Could you rethink design or method to reduce costs?
- Have you got the balance right between what you do yourself and what you buy in from others?
- Could you extend payment terms from your suppliers?

But do be realistic. If you're overly optimistic it will come back to bite you when the project fails to deliver those promised returns. Because if you go ahead, you should take the time at a later date to review whether the project met (or possibly exceeded) the financial expectations.

Whilst it may be difficult to accurately isolate every incremental cash flow that has happened as a result of implementing a project it's worth looking back and having an open discussion about where your predictions were sound and where they were not.

This should not be a finger-pointing exercise. Far from it. It should be an opportunity to learn from the experience to understand how it can be done even better next time.

Dictionary of Accounting Jargon

Accruals are costs that have been 'incurred' but not yet paid for but which, under the *matching principle*, must be included in the calculation of profit.

Amortisation, like *depreciation*, is a way of, for the purpose of calculating profit, spreading the cost of certain *fixed assets* over their useful life to the business.

Attributable costs are those costs associated with the products or services that have been sold – see *matching principle*.

Balance Sheet is a statement at a point in time of where the money to finance the business came from and where it is currently invested – see Chapter 2.

CAPEX is a term that often refers not just to *capital expenditure* but also the approval process – see Chapter 8.

Capital expenditure is the purchase of *fixed assets*.

Carrying amount is an alternative term for NBV.

Cash flow is the increase or decrease in the amount of cash held.

Cash Flow Statement analyses the cash flows arising from operating, financing and investment activities in the business. The statement can be used to reconcile the difference between profit and cash flow – see Chapter 4.

Consignment stock may be supplier's stock, often held on your premises, that can be called off as and when required. The stock only becomes 'yours' (and therefore your investment and your risk) as and when you need it. Conversely, your customers may require you to hold consignment stock for them.

Contribution is the difference between the selling price and the variable cost of a product or service – see p.91.

Cost of Goods Sold (COGS) is an alternative term for *Cost of Sales*.

Cost of Sales are the costs directly associated with making the products or delivering the services that have been sold (e.g. labour, materials and running costs) - see p.35.

Cost rate is the rate applied to product or service costs to allow for overheads or shared costs – see p.89.

Creditors is an alternative name for *payables*.

Current assets is the sum invested in *inventory*, *receivables* and cash - see p.132.

Current liabilities is the money owed to others (e.g. suppliers) that is due to be paid within 12 months – see p.132.

Debtors is an alternative name for *receivables*.

Depreciation is a charge against profit each year for the cost of providing business capability through the investment in *fixed assets* – see p.128.

Discounted Cash Flow (DCF) adjusts future *cash flows* to their *net present values* by applying the relevant *discount factors* – see p.105.

Discount factors are the opposite of compound interest factors and are used to discount future money flows into their equivalents in 'today's money' – see Appendix 7.

Earnings are the profits left over for shareholders after all other costs have been met – see p.36.

Earnings Before Interest and Tax (EBIT) is another term for *operating profit*.

Earnings Before Interest, Tax, Depreciation and Amortisation (EBITDA) is calculated by adding the *depreciation* and *amortisation* charges back to *EBIT* - see p.37 and p.51.

Earnings Per Share (EPS) is a measure of performance of the shareholders' investment – see p.71.

Fixed assets are items purchased with the intention of keeping them and using them over a number of years to provide a capability to make products or deliver services.

Fixed costs are costs that do not vary with the volume of output – e.g. rent.

Gearing measures the relative proportions of capital supplied by shareholders as distinct from lenders - see p.71.

Gross Profit is the difference between the sales value and the *cost of sales* – see p.35.

Income Statement is an alternative name for the *Profit and Loss Account*.

Incremental cost is the additional or marginal cost.

Internal Rate of Return (IRR) is the discount rate at which an overall project *Net Present Value* is zero – see p.108.

Inventory is the sum of money invested in raw materials, work-in-progress (WIP) and finished goods.

Loans are sources of long-term funding for which there is a contractual obligation to make the agreed interest payments and capital repayments – see Appendix 2.

Marginal cost is the additional cost incurred and is a term often used in relation to the extra cost of producing one more unit of output – see p.97.

Matching principle is used to make the profit figure meaningful by stating that the value of sales must be compared to the costs associated with those sales regardless of whether payments for these resources (such as materials and labour) have or have not yet been made – see p.39.

Net Assets Employed (NAE) is the total investment in *fixed assets* and *working capital* – see p.13.

Net Book Value (NBV) is the value at which *fixed assets* are stated on the *Balance Sheet* being the purchase price less the cumulative *depreciation* charged to date – see p.25.

Net Capital Employed (NCE) is the amount of long-term finance invested in the business comprising share capital, reserves and loans – see p.12.

Net Current Assets is an alternative name for *working capital*.

Net Present Value (NPV) is the value of a *cash flow* in 'today's money'. Projects covering a number of years can be evaluated by applying *discount factors* to future cash flows thereby allowing for the 'time value' of those flows – see p.106.

Net worth is an alternative name for *shareholders' funds*.

Nominal value of a share is the value shown on the face of the share certificate as distinct from the current price at which shares are being bought and sold.

Non-current Assets is an alternative name for *fixed assets*.

Operating Profit is the difference between the sales value and all the business costs but before the financing costs of interest, tax and dividend – see p.35.

Overhead rate is an alternative term for *cost rate*.

Payables is the amount of money owed to suppliers for goods or services that have been received but have not yet been paid for.

Payback is the time taken for a project to recoup the initial outlay – see p.104.

Prepayments are costs that have been paid but, as their 'value' has not yet been 'received', to comply with the *matching principle*, are excluded from the calculation of profit.

Profit & Loss Account details the sales, costs and profit for the business over a specific period of time – see Chapter 3.

Profitability is a measure of the amount of profit made relative to how much had to be invested to earn that profit – see p.62.

Profit After Tax (PAT) is an alternative term for *earnings*.

Profit Before Tax (PBT) is *Operating Profit* less interest costs – see p.35.

Receivables is the amount of money owed by customers for goods or services they have received but have not yet paid for.

Reserves is a collective term for financial gains made by the business that belong to the shareholders and therefore form part of *shareholders' funds*. Included in reserves is the business' cumulative *retained profit* – see p.23.

Retained Earnings is an alternative term for *retained profit*.

Retained Profit is the profit available to reinvest back into the business after all costs have been met – see p.16.

Return On Capital Employed (ROCE) is a measure of *profitability* – see p.63.

Revenue is an alternative term for the value of invoiced sales.

Revenue expenditure is expenditure on running costs (i.e. all operating costs excluding the purchase of *fixed assets*).

Sensitivity analysis helps assess risk by recalculating proposals on a 'what if' basis to ascertain the factors that are critical to success.

Share capital comprises the number of shares in issue valued at their *nominal value*.

Shareholders' funds is the total long-term finance provided by shareholders and comprises *share capital* and *reserves* – see p.23.

Standard costs are usually set at the start of each financial year and normally reflect expected cost levels for material, labour and overhead costs – see Appendix 8.

Statement of Financial Position is an alternative name for a *Balance Sheet*.

Stock is an alternative name for *inventory*.

Total Equity is an alternative name for *shareholders' funds*.

Turnover is an alternative term for the value of invoiced sales.

Variable costs are costs that vary with the volume of output – e.g. materials.

Variance is the difference between a standard and actual cost – see p.147.

Working Capital is the net investment in *current assets* and *current liabilities*.

Working Capital Cycle is the flow of *working capital* from cash back into cash again as the business makes, delivers and sells its products or services – see Appendix 4.

Written-Down Value (WDV) is an alternative term for *NBV*.

Appendix 1

Share Capital

One of the ways to provide the business with long-term capital is to attract investors to buy shares. (With a new business these may initially be friends and relations but could eventually be the general public.)

Why does anyone buy shares?
To make money.

How do you make money out of owning shares?
You hope (note this important 4-letter word) to make an income from your investment when the company pays a dividend. You also hope (there it goes again) your investment will grow in value allowing you to eventually sell the shares for more than they cost.

What is the relationship between shareholders and the business? Are they, like the providers of loans, "third-party cold-blooded outsiders"? (see p.124.)
Far from it. The shareholders own the business. When someone buys a share, what they are really buying is part ownership of that business. Of course we know that – but it is very easy to lose sight of this when working in a large organisation. Here you see your boss, and your boss' boss ... and sitting there at the top of the organisation, the Chief Exec and Board of Directors. From within the business it feels like they own it. After all, who decides whether we bid for the new contract, develop the new product or service, take people on or downsize, move work to another location? But the shareholders own the business and they

appoint the top team to run the business on their behalf.

What can the shareholders do if they don't like the decisions the board are making?

Replace them. Which explains why the board will want to keep the shareholders happy by running the business in such a way that they can deliver dividends and share price growth.

Share Price

What may individual shareholders do with their shares if they feel their investment is not performing well and are unable or unwilling to muster sufficient support to replace that top team?

Sell them.

What happens to the share price if people start to sell their shares?

It falls. A simple case of supply and demand. If more people want to buy than sell, the share price rises. If more want to sell than buy, the price falls. And what do companies become vulnerable to if their share price falls? Takeover. Because when one company buys another it doesn't buy the land, buildings, plant, equipment, inventory... although that's what it gets!- it buys the shares. Because if you own the shares you own the business. So if the share price falls the price tag for the business reduces, attracting potential predators.

So, share prices are determined purely and simply by supply and demand. But what about that statement accountants prepare called the Balance Sheet that lists the value of everything the company owns... the land, buildings, equipment, inventory...? Surely if you take that total value and divide it by the number of shares that must be the share price?

No. When you buy a share, you don't just buy a fraction of the things the company owns. What you are really buying is a share of the company's future financial performance. A share of its creativity to take the things it owns and use them to make goods or organise services and deliver them to a market and in so doing generate a stream of sales, profits and cash into the future.

Not all "assets" of the business are to be found on the Balance Sheet. For example, what do companies say time and time again is their biggest asset?

Their people. But we don't 'value' people and put them on the Balance Sheet (and perhaps interestingly therefore have to deal with the issue of how we should "depreciate" them over their useful life to the business....)

And what about the order book? When a company announces that it has won a large order what is likely to happen to the share price? It will probably go up as investors rush to buy into that future success. But nothing may yet have happened to affect the Balance Sheet. The business may not have even started to buy the necessary materials.

So, the share price is all about expectation and investors' opinions of the future financial performance of the business.

Which helps explain why share prices can be so volatile. And that volatility can create other false impressions about the financial position of the business.

You hear people say that as their company's share price is high the business must have lots of money around for salary increases and bonuses.

Not necessarily.

Take a simple example.

Alf has a great business idea. All he needs is £10,000 of capital. He approaches his friend Bert and persuades him to buy 10,000 £1 shares in the new business. Bert hands over the £10,000, Alf hands over the 10,000 share certificates and uses the £10,000 to rent some premises, buy some equipment ... and the business is up and running very successfully.

A year or so later Cecilia bumps into Bert and, having heard how well the business is doing (and knowing that Bert is about to move house and could do with releasing some cash), offers to buy the shares from Bert for £15,000. Not a bad return thinks Bert. So they shake hands and the deal is struck. The share price has risen from £1 to £1.50 but look what happens. Bert hands over the share certificates to Cecilia and Cecilia hands over the £15,000 to Bert. No extra money comes into the business. Alf just has the initial £10,000 that he has put to work in the business.

Donald dabbles in shares and he has heard on the grapevine that the business Alf is running is about to win a large order. So he offers to buy the shares from Cecilia for £2 per share. Note again what happens. Cecilia hands over the share certificates to Donald and Donald gives the £20,000 to Cecilia. The share price is now at twice its original value ... and yet there has been no increase in the share capital invested in the business.

Sadly, there is always one fall-guy in this and the large order goes dreadfully wrong. Ellie, a bit of a business-angel, who likes investing in struggling businesses offers to buy the shares from Donald for £1 each. Donald just wants out so the deal is struck. Ellie hands over the £10,000 to Donald and Donald hands her the share certificates. The share price has collapsed – and yet there is no reduction in the amount of capital invested in the business.

So, despite the dramatic headlines that accompany announcements of upswings or downturns in the stock market, increases or decreases in the value of shares do not affect the financial position of the business – what they do affect is the personal wealth of those fortunate (or unfortunate) enough to have been caught holding those bits of paper called share certificates.

[Of course, there are repercussions for the business of movements in share price. If they are rising, owners of the shares will be pleased with their investment and may be willing to put additional capital into the business should there be opportunities for growth. Banks too will be influenced in their lending decisions (and the risk they attach to them as reflected by the interest rates they charge on loans) by the confidence investors have in the future performance of the business as evidenced by the share price.]

Raising Additional Share Capital

Take the example of a business that issues 100,000 new shares. The shares have a nominal value (the value shown on the share certificate) of say £1 but will be sold at the current market price of for example £5. What will happen to the share price when the new shares are issued? Will it go up? Go down? Stay more or less the same? It can do any of these as it all depends on what the market believes the business will achieve with the additional £500,000 of capital.

As far as accounting for new share issues is concerned, share capital on the Balance Sheet is valued at its nominal value so "premiums" have to be accounted for elsewhere. In the example above cash will increase by £500,000 (top half of the Balance Sheet) but Share Capital (bottom half of the Balance Sheet), which is always shown at its nominal value, will only increase by £100,000. The problem is resolved by creating a "Share Premium Account" in which to put the £400,000 premium paid for the shares and which is included on the Balance Sheet under the heading "Reserves" (see p.23).

Appendix 2

Loans

Most businesses use loans as one of the ways to provide the long-term finance needed to support the investment in *Fixed Assets* and *Working Capital*. There's nothing wrong with borrowing money to help finance a business; most companies do just that. But there is everything wrong with borrowing too much money.

If you approach a potential lender for a loan, the first thing they will want to see is the business plan and, as businesses go to the wall not because they make a loss but because they run out of cash, they will look particularly carefully at your cash flow projections.

[If you're not sure why profit and cash flow are not the same thing take a look at Chapter 4, The Cash Flow Statement].

If they like the look of the business plan (and believe you have the managerial skills to deliver it) they may agree to lend the money.

Their business model is to make money out of lending money so they're going to be charging interest on the loan – and expecting repayment of the capital at some agreed future date.

When the business takes on a loan it signs a contract committing to make the agreed payments as and when they fall due. To make sure these terms are adhered to the lender will look for some form of security or collateral. If the business is unable to invest the money it has borrowed profitably, to generate the profits and cash to make the agreed payments, the lender may come in, sell off some of the business assets to recover the debt and there may be no business left.

This is 'third-party cold-blooded contractual money'. So borrowers need to be careful. Borrowing money increases the financial risk to the business. This shouldn't put you off borrowing money – but it should make you wary of just how much should be borrowed.

The relative proportions in which businesses are financed by loans as distinct from shareholder investment is referred to as gearing and is explained on p.71.

Appendix 3

Fixed Assets (or Non-current Assets)

What Are They?
If you make a list of all the things your business needs you'll find the items fall into two distinct categories. Some purchases are of a 'one-off' nature (e.g. equipment) whereas others are constantly consumed and replaced (e.g. materials). This appendix looks at the first category, known as Fixed Assets. These items (purchased through the Capital Expenditure process) are bought with the intention of keeping them.

[By contrast, items in the second category are purchased with the intention of pulling them through the business as fast as you can by turning them into the products or services your customers are willing to pay for. To learn more about this take a look at Appendix 4, Working Capital.]

Bought with the intention of keeping them? Why would you do this? Surely business is about buying items and selling them on at a profit?

The reason you buy fixed assets is because you're going to use them. They give you the capability of turning materials into the products or services the market wants. They provide the 'facilities', the 'processes', the 'tools to do the job'. Without them you could not make your products or deliver your services

A Strategic Choice
The authorisation process to gain approval to buy fixed assets can be

extremely onerous (see Chapter 8, Capital Expenditure Appraisal). It is often assumed that this is just because items tend to be high-value. But it is more than this. When you choose your 'capability' you make a strategic decision that defines how you are going to do business. When you choose your land and buildings, you geographically locate your business. When you select equipment, you define the process you are going to use to turn materials into products or services. When you select your vehicles, you determine your distribution strategy. If you get these decisions wrong and your competitor gets them right, it can put you out of business. It is the cost to the business of getting it wrong that results in a capital expenditure appraisal process that is so challenging.

For most businesses the market sets the price for products or services based on the customer's perceived value of what is on offer. Customers care about the product or service that they receive, not about how cost-effectively their supplier has gone about their business. The customer will not pay a premium for your offering just because you choose to make it inefficiently and therefore wastefully. It is therefore up to you to keep focused on the market and continually align your business to meeting market needs in the most efficient way. You 'sell' these fixed assets to your customer in just the same way as you sell the materials you've used; both are integral aspects of the product or service they are purchasing. If you get it right, the customer will buy your products or services at a price that covers all your costs – including the cost of providing this capability.

The accountant's jargon of referring to these items as "fixed" assets may be unhelpful and misleading here. To most people 'fixed' implies something that doesn't change. This should not be the case with fixed assets and is not the impression accountants intend to convey. If there's any word that should be buzzing round businesses these days it's the word "challenge". This challenge applies to your fixed assets just as much as to anything else. As the market changes, it is important that your business continually realigns itself, looking for better ways of doing more with less. Standing still is rarely a sustainable option. It may take time and money to restructure your 'capability' but just shrugging your shoulders and making the best of a bad job is unlikely to be a realistic option.

Accounting Treatment

All accountants mean when they refer to certain assets as being "fixed" is that when they were purchased, it was believed these items would continue to bring value (in terms of a capability to make products or deliver services the market wants) to the business over a number of years and would therefore need to be accounted for differently.

If you want your profit figure to be meaningful you will want to compare the selling price for your products or services with a fair assessment of the costs that have been incurred in making them. It would therefore not be sensible to put all the cost of a fixed asset into the profit calculation in the year of purchase (and nothing into the other years that will also benefit from its use), as this would distort the results.

Profit would look dreadful in the year of purchase and artificially good for those subsequent years that were not carrying a 'fair' share of the costs. The accountant therefore spreads the cost of these fixed assets over their useful life and feeds a fair share into your business costs each year.

Take, for example, the purchase of a new piece of equipment costing £50,000 to be used to deliver a product or service (and therefore to help generate sales revenue) for the next 5 years. Rather than putting all the £50,000 cost into the calculation of profit in the first year and nothing into the following four years, the cost is spread fairly over the 5-year life of the asset and charged against profit each year as "depreciation" or "amortisation".

If the accountant used a "straight-line" method for depreciating the equipment, there would be a depreciation charge of £10,000 included as one of the business costs in each of the 5 years.

$$\frac{\text{Purchase price of equipment}}{\text{Useful life (Years)}} = \frac{£50,000}{5 \text{ years}} = £10,000 \text{ p.a.}$$

(Note that this is nothing to do with any financing decision to spread the payments for purchasing an asset over a number of years. That is a conversation about cash. Here we are talking about cost.)

As far as the Balance Sheet is concerned, fixed assets are valued at their cost less the cumulative depreciation charged to date. This "net" value is referred to as "Written-Down Value" (WDV), "Net Book Value" (NBV) or "Carrying amount".

In the case of the equipment in this example it would be valued for Balance Sheet purposes as follows:

	Year 1 £	**Year 2** £	**Year 3** £	**Year 4** £	**Year 5** £
Cost	50,000	50,000	50,000	50,000	50,000
Cumulative Depreciation	10,000	20,000	30,000	40,000	50,000
NBV	40,000	30,000	20,000	10,000	0

For an explanation of some of the implications of the way fixed assets are accounted for and valued, see Chapter 2, Balance Sheet.

Appendix 4

Working Capital

Businesses buy in materials, spend money converting them into products or services and then sell them to their customers. Cash flows out of the business and then back in again. And, if you've got it right and can sell your products or services at a profit, the cash that eventually flows in exceeds the cash that you had to outlay.

But businesses rarely complete this process instantaneously. Unless you buy materials for cash, turn them into products or services and sell them for cash all on the same day, then at any point in time there will be money 'trapped' in your cash-to-cash cycle. And this investment, referred to as Working Capital, has to be financed.

The scale of the investment you need will depend on the way 'time' works in your business and the volume of products or services working their way round the cycle. It's helpful to look at the cycle one step at a time, starting with Cash.

The Working Capital Cycle

Cash is used to buy materials ....

that are then converted using people and other resources through work-in-progress or work-in-process (WIP) into finished goods or services.

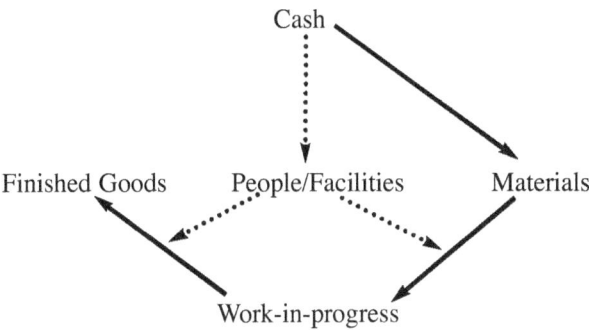

These goods or services are then delivered to customers ..

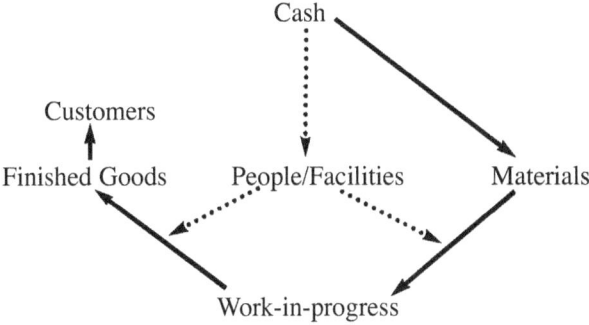

who will, after taking any agreed credit period, pay for them.

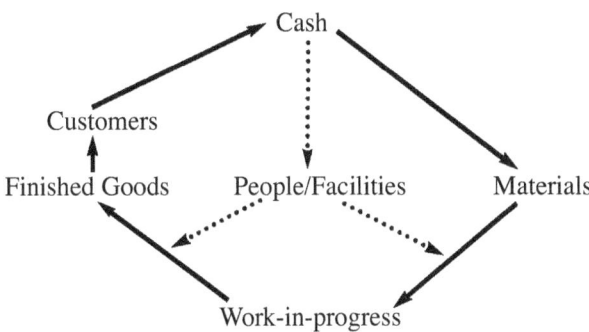

The amount of money tied up in this cycle of Cash back into Cash again is referred to by accountants as Current Assets.

For most businesses, life is fortunately not that simple as they rarely pay cash for materials. Instead, they negotiate credit from their suppliers. So a supplier delivers to the business which then runs as fast and furiously round the cycle as far as it can get ....

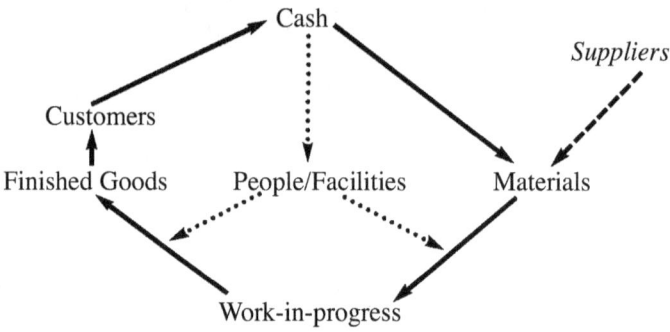

before having to pay the supplier's invoice.

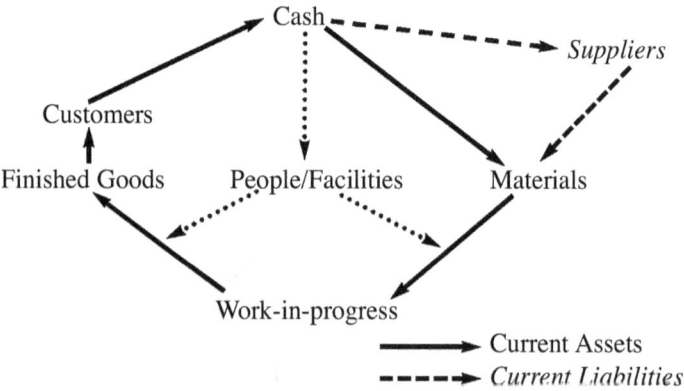

This allows the business to finance some of their Current Assets using other peoples' money. Accountants refer to such credit as Current Liabilities.

Therefore the amount of investment the business needs to find to finance the Working Capital cycle is:

Working Capital = Current Assets − Current Liabilities

(When accountants talk of "current" assets or liabilities they mean cash or things that will result in cash being received or paid out in the short-term.)

Time is Money
How much working capital the business needs is determined by time. Look back at the cycle and consider the example of a supermarket buying in some tinned beans from their supplier on 60 days credit.

No such thing as raw material or WIP, the tin goes straight on to the shelf in the store.

How long do goods sit on the shelf of a supermarket? Perhaps a couple of days. So, with 58 days left before the supermarket has to pay its suppliers, along comes the customer with his shopping trolley.

How many days credit have customers negotiated with their local supermarket? Even if they pay by cheque or credit card it is cash to the business almost straight away. What a lovely world to live in!

If only time worked the same way in all businesses ...
A manufacturer of seals for the automotive sector also buys materials on 60 days credit from their suppliers. The processes the seals have to go through means that it takes about 30 days to finish the products that are then shipped out to customers who tend to pay on 30 day terms. Can you see how the business is receiving the cash for its products around the same time as it is paying its suppliers?

Then there is the manufacturer of complex components for the aerospace market. They too negotiate 60 days credit from their suppliers, but it takes about 6 months to manufacture their product so they have to finance it themselves throughout most of this time. They then deliver the components to customers who have negotiated payment terms often in excess of 120 days. Can you see the impact that 'time' has on the scale of the investment required by a business such as this?

Accounting Terminology

As far as the jargon is concerned, accountants refer to the total amount trapped in raw materials, WIP and finished goods as inventory (or stock). The amount you're waiting to receive from your customers is known as receivables (or debtors) and the amount you owe other people (e.g. suppliers) is known as payables (or creditors).

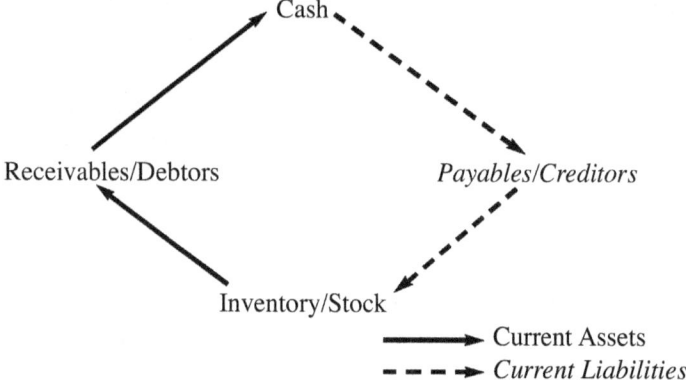

Hence the investment in working capital is:

   Working Capital = (Inventory + Receivables + Cash) − Payables

Accounting Treatment

Under the accounting principle of prudency where accountants are required to take a conservative approach when valuing assets (see Chapter 2, The Balance Sheet), the components of working capital are valued as follows:

Inventory − at the <u>lower</u> of cost or net realisable value (what it could be sold for).
Receivables − at the amount believed to be collectable (i.e. excluding those invoices at risk of becoming bad debts).
Creditors − the amount owed
Cash − the sum of money in cash and at the bank.

For a more detailed explanation of the way working capital is valued and the implications of 'writing down' assets, see Chapter 2, The Balance Sheet.

Pedal Power

There is only one word on the cycle that accountants like.
Cash. Cash is king!
Accountants can do things with cash (pay people their wages and salaries, pay suppliers, pay the bank their interest, pay the taxman ...). They can't do this with anything else on the cycle. Everything else on the journey represents risk.

So how can you lure accountants to take on this risk?
There's one thing accountants like more than cash.
More cash.

If you are in business delivering a product or service on which you make a profit, every time you set out on the journey round the cycle and complete it successfully, you end up with more cash than you started with. Now you've got the accountants' attention. But there are still a few issues you'll need to focus on.

Don't stop till you get there!
There is only one step of the cycle that brings any real financial benefit to the business. The customer paying you. You invoice the customer when you ship the product or deliver the service – but all you are doing at this stage is transferring your resources into someone else's warehouse. Only when the customer pays you do you arrive at your destination. If you fail to complete this final step you may as well have saved yourself a load of time and effort and just sat in the corner of the office dropping £50 notes into the shredding machine. It's not just down to accountants to collect the cash after everyone else has moved on to getting the next contract fulfilled. You need to make sure that everyone understands that the job isn't finished until the customer pays for the work that has been done.

Don't hang around!
As soon as you move out of Cash, and embark on the hazardous journey

round the cycle, you bring risk into the business. Any order commitment with your suppliers just makes this risk worse.

What if the market changes and you're caught holding money tied up in materials, goods or services that nobody wants? What if you need to modify your design? What if your customer goes out of business before he pays you?

It makes sense to plan the way you run your business so that you can whiz through the cycle as fast as you can to minimise the risk of being caught out if the circumstances change – and maximise the speed with which you can respond to opportunities such as stepping in to help a customer out when a competitor lets them down or where there is a sudden upturn in the market.

And as the faster you go round the cycle the less money you have trapped at any point in time, and as every £1 had to come from somewhere, that means lower financing costs – and therefore more profit!

Don't mess up!
Whilst it's great to think that every time you pedal around the cycle and complete it successfully you're going to generate profit and cash for the business, be honest with yourself, do you always get everything you do 'right first time'? Your customer rewards you for the things you get right; you pay the price when you get it wrong. Every time you stumble on your journey (for example by buying the wrong materials, or having to rectify work or repeat activities) you are incurring cost that your customer is not going to pay for. Again, that's akin to sitting in the office dropping £50 notes into the shredding machine. What a waste.

Appendix 5

Alternative Balance Sheet Formats

Format 1 (as used in the text – see Chapter 2)

	£	£
Fixed Assets		290,000
Working Capital		
Current Assets	285,000	
Less:		
Current Liabilities	<u>75,000</u>	
		<u>210,000</u>
<u>Net Assets Employed</u>		£500,000
Share Capital	48,000	
Retained Profits (or Reserves)	<u>252,000</u>	
Net Worth		300,000
Loans		<u>200,000</u>
<u>Net Capital Employed</u>		£500,000

Format 2

	£	£
Assets		
Non-current Assets[1]		290,000
Current Assets		285,000
Total Assets		£575,000
Equity and Liabilities		
Share Capital	48,000	
Reserves[2]	252,000	
Total Equity[3]		300,000
Loans		200,000
Current Liabilities		75,000
Total Equity and Liabilities		£575,000

Format 3

	£	£
Fixed Assets		290,000
Current Assets	285,000	
Current Liabilities	75,000	
Net Current Assets		210,000
Total Assets less Current liabilities		500,000
Loans		200,000
Net Assets		£300,000
Capital and Reserves[4]:		
Share Capital		48,000
Reserves		252,000
		£300,000

[1] Another term for Fixed Assets
[2] A collective term which includes Retained Profits (see p.23)
[3] Another term for Net Worth or Shareholders' Funds
[4] Another term for Net Worth or Shareholders' Funds

Appendix 6

Cash Flow Statement - Worked Example

Cash Flow Statement from p.50.

	£
Operating Profit	100,000
Depreciation	25,000
EBITDA	125,000
Increase in Inventory	(22,000)
Increase in Receivables	(29,000)
Increase in Payables	8,000
Cash Flow from Operating Activities	82,000
Interest Paid	(20,000)
Tax Paid	(12,000)
Capital Expenditure	(30,000)
Dividends Paid	(28,000)
Increase in Share Capital	3,000
(Decrease) in Cash	(5,000)

Overleaf is some information you'll need if you want to work through the details behind this Cash Flow Statement.

Profit and Loss Account for the Year Ended 31st December 20XX

	£
Sales	1,000,000
Cost of Sales	700,000
Gross Profit	300,000
Distribution costs	85,000
Administration expenses	115,000
Operating Profit	100,000
Interest	20,000
Profit Before Tax	80,000
Tax	16,000
Profit After Tax	64,000
Dividends	30,000
Retained Profit	34,000

Balance Sheet as at 31st December 20XX

	Previous Year		Current Year	
	£	£	£	£
Fixed Assets:				
Land and buildings		165,000		165,000
Equipment[1]		120,000		125,000
		285,000		290,000
Current Assets:				
Inventory		78,000		100,000
Receivables		151,000		180,000
Cash		10,000		5,000
		239,000		285,000
Current Liabilities:				
Trade Creditors[2]	35,000		43,000	
Interest	1,000		1,000	
Tax	12,000		16,000	
Dividend	13,000		15,000	
	61,000		75,000	
Working Capital		178,000		210,000
Net Assets Employed[3]		£463,000		£500,000
Share Capital	45,000		48,000	
Retained Profits[4]	218,000		252,000	
Net Worth		263,000		300,000
Loans		200,000		200,000
Net Capital Employed		£463,000		£500,000

1 The increase of £5,000 during the year comprises:
- Purchase of new equipment (CAPEX) £30,000
- Depreciation of all equipment £25,000

2 The amount owed to suppliers

3 Net Assets Employed = Fixed Assets + Working Capital

4 As this is a cumulative figure, the increase of £34,000 between the two statements is the retained profit for the year (see Profit and Loss Account above)

The following sections will take you step-by-step through the workings behind the Cash Flow Statement shown on p139.

Cash Flow From Operating Activities

Start by working out how much cash has actually flowed in and out in arriving at the Operating Profit stage of the Profit and Loss Account (P&L).

If the sales invoiced during the period are £1,000,000 (see P&L) and receivables have increased by £29,000 (see movement on Balance Sheet from £151,000 to £180,000) then the amount of cash that has been collected from customers must be £971,000.

If the cost of the goods or services that have been sold is £700,000 (see P&L) and during this period inventory levels increased by £22,000 (from £78,000 to £100,000 as per Balance Sheet) then the cost incurred must have been £722,000. Included in the £700,000 cost is £25,000 depreciation (see footnote 1) that doesn't involve any cash flow so the cash that could potentially have been paid out for materials, labour and overhead is £697,000 (i.e. £722,000 - £25,000). If this is added to the cost of distribution and administration from the P&L of £200,000, there is a potential cash outflow of £897,000.

But if you look on the Balance Sheet you will see that the trade creditors figure increased by £8,000 (from £35,000 to £43,000). The business increased the amount of credit it was taking from its suppliers. Therefore the actual amount of cash paid out was not the £897,000 just calculated above, but £8,000 less than this, i.e. £889,000.

If you then compare the figures that you've just calculated for cash collected of £971,000 and cash paid out of £889,000 you'll have a net figure for the Cash Flow from Operating Activities of £82,000.

On the Cash Flow Statement these adjustments are encapsulated by taking EBITDA and the movements in Working Capital from the Balance Sheet.

	£
Operating Profit	100,000
Depreciation	25,000
EBITDA	125,000
Increase in Inventory	(22,000)
Increase in Receivables	(29,000)
Increase in Payables	8,000
Cash Flow from Operating Activities	82,000

Interest Paid

The interest owed at the start of the financial year is £1,000 (see Balance Sheet). During the year interest costs are £20,000 (see P&L) and £1,000 is owing at the end of the financial year (see Balance Sheet).

The amount paid is therefore:

	£
Amount owed at start of year	1,000
+ Amount charged in the year	20,000
- Amount owed at the end of the year	1,000
Amount paid	20,000

Tax Paid

The interest owed at the start of the financial year is £12,000 (see Balance Sheet). During the year tax costs are £16,000 (see P&L) and £16,000 is owing at the end of the financial year (see Balance Sheet).

The amount paid is therefore:

	£
Amount owed at start of year	12,000
+ Amount charged in the year	16,000
- Amount owed at the end of the year	16,000
Amount paid	12,000

Capital Expenditure

The amount paid for new equipment was £30,000 (see note 1 to Balance Sheet).

Dividend Paid

The dividend owed at the start of the financial year is £13,000 (see Balance Sheet). During the year dividend costs are £30,000 (see P&L) and £15,000 is owing at the end of the financial year (see Balance Sheet).

The amount paid is therefore:

	£
Amount owed at start of year	13,000
+ Amount charged in the year	30,000
- Amount owed at the end of the year	15,000
Amount paid	28,000

Share Capital

Share Capital increases from £45,000 to £48,000 (see Balance Sheet) raising an additional £3,000 cash.

Cash Flow

The statement balances to the £5,000 decrease in cash during the year (from £10,000 to £5,000 see Balance Sheet).

Appendix 7

Discounted Cash Flows

For the purposes of this explanation, assume interest rates are 10%.

If you were offered the choice of £1,000 now or £1,000 in a year's time which one are you going to choose? The £1,000 now – and not just because the giver might change their minds!

If you took the money now and put it in the bank you would have £1,100 by the end of the year.

So £1,000 now and £1,000 in a year's time are not worth the same to you. If on the other hand you were offered £1,000 now or £1,100 in a year's time there would be no rational reason for preferring one over the other – they would be 'worth' the same amount.

If you left the money on deposit, by the end of the second year you would have £1,210 (i.e. £1,100 + 10% or £1,100 x 110/100); the third year £1,331 (i.e. £1,210 + 10% or £1,210 x 110/100); and so on.

So if interest rates are 10% then £1,000 now or £1,331 in three years' time are worth the same amount. If you were to offer one person £1,000 and another £1,331 in three years' time you would be treating them equally.

When looking at project appraisal, instead of compounding cash flows to a future point in time, the opposite is done. By 'flipping over' the compounding factor (in this case 110/100 becomes 100/110) future cash flows are discounted back to their 'present value' – i.e. their equivalent in 'money today'. This then allows these present values to be compared with the cost of going ahead with the project (a cash outlay 'today') to see whether the project is financially worthwhile.

If a project offers a cash inflow of £1,000 in one year's time, that's worth the same to you as being given a cheque today for:

£1,000 x 100/110 = £909

[You know that's right because if you go into the bank today with £909 and earn 10% interest, when you check your statement in a year's time you will have £1,000.]

So £1,000 in one year's time is worth the same thing to you as being given £909 today. In other words, if interest rates are 10% then £909 is the "present value" of £1,000 in one year's time.

What about a project that rather than paying out £1,000 in one year's time, pays it out in two years' time? How much is that £1,000 worth in 'today's money terms'?

£1,000 x 100/110 x 100/110   = £ 826

Run it through your calculator to check. If you put £826 in the bank now and earn compound interest at 10% on it for two years you end up with £1,000 in your account. So if interest rates are 10%, the present value of £1,000 in two years' time is £826.

You've now established the "discount factors" to be applied to future money if interest rates are 10% :

One year's time :   1 x 100/110   = 0.909
Two year's time :   1 x 100/110 x 100/110 = 0.826

The good news is that you don't have to bash away on a calculator for hours to establish these discount factors – they're readily available in tables covering different interest rates and much longer timescales.
Just choose the rate you need and enter the factors into your calculation.

On the next page is the example from p.106.

	NCF	**Discount Factor**	**NPV**
	£	10%	£
Year 1	80,000	0.909	72,720
Year 2	150,000	0.826	123,900
Year 3	90,000	0.751	67,590
			264,210
		Initial Investment	250,000
		Project NPV	14,210

In Year 1, the cash inflow of £80,000 has a NPV of £72,720.
So if interest rates are 10%, the cash inflow the project will generate of £80,000 in one year's time is equivalent to being given a cheque today for £72,720.

Continue with the same argument for Years 2 and 3 then take a look at that total NPV for the three years of £264,210. This tells you that going ahead with a project that results in cash inflows of £80,000 in Year 1 then £150,000 in Year 2 and £90,000 in Year 3, is worth the same thing as being given a cheque today for £264,210.

Would you be willing to outlay £250,000 to go ahead with a project that would give you benefits equivalent to being given a cheque today for £264,210?
The rational answer is yes. The business would be £14,210 'better off' if you proceed with the project.

Appendix 8

Standard Costing

Standard costing is often used in conjunction with overhead absorption costing systems. "Standards" are set, usually at the beginning of the financial year, and are the expected or forecast costs.

There are usually:

- standard costs for the purchase price of materials;
- standard usage for that material;
- standard times for tasks to be carried out;
- standard rates at which people are to be paid to carry out those tasks;
- and a standard *overhead rate* to be applied to that work and those materials.

As with any forecast, all will not go according to plan. Actual costs incurred will not always match with those standards thereby creating "variances". Some of those variances will be favourable – e.g. purchasing materials at a cheaper price than forecast. Some will be adverse – e.g. taking longer to carry out a task than was predicted.

All actual costs are analysed into standards and variances with the inventory continuing on its journey through the business at its standard value with all the variances being 'thrown into a bucket' to be reported on separately.

The merits of such an approach are that where there are lots of different parts running through a business with the same part being used on different contracts it simplifies cost control and that the variance reports allows the management team to focus on 'exceptions'.

As external financial reports require inventory to be reported at actual rather than standard cost, an adjustment will be made to the value of inventory to include those variances that relate to costs that are still 'in the business'. Those variances that are attributed to goods or services that have been 'despatched' will adjust the cost of sales from standard to actual and will therefore be shown in the Profit and Loss Account.

(In reality, if the inventory value is low and the variances are small, this adjustment from standard to actual may not take place.)

Appendix 9

Product Life-Cyles

Here is a simplified life-cycle for a product:

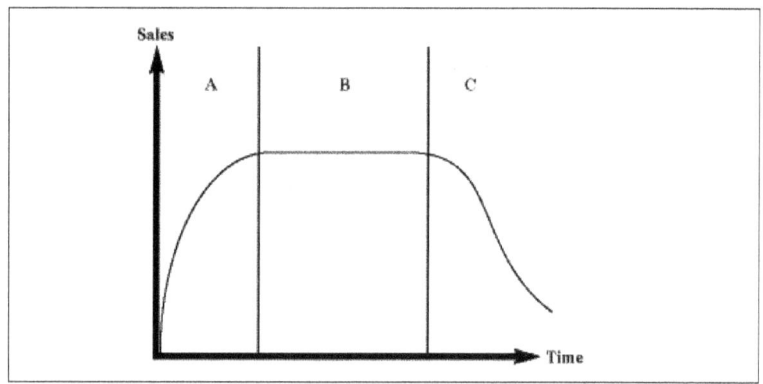

The 'A' stage, as you launch the new product, is often known as the "star"; products in the 'B' stage where you are selling in steady, relatively high volumes are spoken of as "cows"; and in the 'C' stage when demand for the product declines, products may be referred to as "dogs".

The financial performance of the business will be influenced by where your products are on that cycle.

Cash Flow
Look at the 5 levers (see p.53) that determine whether cash flows in or out of your business.

EBITDA
+ Movement in Working Capital:
  Δ Inventory
  Δ Receivables
  Δ Payables
+ <u>Capital Expenditure</u>
= Cash Flow

'A' Stage
At this 'rising star' stage profit is usually low as you have the costs of sorting out any teething problems.

Look back at that Working Capital cycle on p.45. The amount invested in the cycle will increase as you feed in cash to get the cycle turning but you will have little, if anything, back from your customers yet. And this is the time when you need to do all that capital expenditure to give yourself the capability to make the new product.

Hence cash tends to pour out of the business at this time. Businesses don't go under because they make a loss. They fail because they run out of cash.

Ironically just as everything looks great and a business is 'on the up' they're also financially extremely vulnerable.

For example, if your sales increase from £10,000 per month to £14,000 a month and credit terms to customers remain unchanged at net 60 days, an additional £8,000 cash will have to be found to finance the increase in receivables resulting from this success.

All too often businesses fail to predict the amount of cash they need to get through the 'A' stage. If they did, they would make sure they had everything organised so that they could get it through it as quickly and cost-effectively as possible (e.g. by making sure the design was sound) and also avoid taking too many products through the 'A' stage at once.

'B' Stage
Products in this stage should be your 'cash cows'. They're called cows because you ought to be able to 'milk' them to generate cash.

What do those cash levers look like now?

Profits should be high as you're now producing a proven product at a steady rate.

As the supply chain is now sorted and processes are under control inventory 'buffers' can be removed.

Credit terms with suppliers are being maintained and now that any quality and delivery issues have been resolved, payments from customers should be flowing in on a regular basis.

As for capital expenditure, there should be little other than the occasional bit of replacement kit.

Cash should be flowing in – and it's the cash from your "cows" that you need for those "stars" that are your future "cows"!

'C' Stage

You need to keep your "dogs" under control and watch those cash levers. Complexity breeds cost and if you fail to adapt your processes to those suitable for smaller volumes you may be making little, if any, profit. Even businesses that claim they "make all their money on spares" rather than original equipment because selling prices for spares are higher may be surprised by how much narrower that differential can be (see the section on costing below).

Well-managed, the investment in working capital should fall (although lemming-like, many fail to spot the edge of the precipice resulting in an initial increase in inventory as the business readjusts the supply chain to the lower levels of demand) and there should be little if any capital expenditure.

When the "dogs" stop generating cash it's time to cut their tails off.

Costing

One of the criticisms of overhead absorption costing (see p.87) is that cost rates fail to discriminate between those products that are easy to produce and those that cause disproportionate hassle.

Cost rates are averages, calculated by taking the total costs of a cost centre and dividing that by the number of hours work that the centre is expected to generate. Think about what goes into the cost of the cost centre. The costs of procurement, receiving, scheduling, supervisory payroll costs, production engineering... Does this example strike a chord with your business?

A range of products, including X and Y, travel through a cost centre that has a cost rate of £60 per hour.

Product X has been around for years. The supply chain works well. X is manufactured in a simple 'drum beat' fashion and sails through the cost centre like a dream. Each unit takes 10 minutes to machine therefore the costing system reports that it 'costs' the company £10 of overhead costs to make a unit of X.

Product Y on the other hand is a nightmare. Poorly designed and in low-demand, the material supplier struggles to produce the quality required. A group of supervisors and engineers huddle round the machine as the most skilled person on the shopfloor tries to nurse the product through the machining process. As it takes 10 minutes per unit to machine, product Y is also reported to have 'cost' the company £10 of overhead.

An extreme case. But inevitably there will be winners and losers from the costing system as a result of cross-subsidisation. Does this matter? It does if it encourages people to take the wrong decisions for the business.

'A' Stage

Products at this stage will typically be under-costed making it harder to justify the appropriate investment in up-front design and methods to make the learning curve faster and cheaper.

Setting targets for 'cost-down initiatives' and measuring whether they are achieved is difficult if the starting point isn't understood. Profit forecasts for periods of new product launch will be overstated and expectations unrealistically high.

'B' Stage

With products almost inevitably over-costed, there is a grave danger of killing off those cash-generating cows.

At this point in the life-cycle there is likely to be strong competition in the market and a downwards pressure on price. If costs are overstated this might encourage companies to pull out of what is, in reality, high-margin cash-generating business.

'C' Stage

At this stage products tend to be under-costed if costing systems fail to pick up the 'hassle' associated with managing variety. As volumes fall this becomes particularly pertinent. Processes that were well-aligned with the market at the 'B' stage might not be so for the 'C' stage and it may be appropriate to re-think how those market needs are met.

Businesses need to make sure that the market continues to pay a price that covers all the costs. Be sceptical when looking at profit margins and watch out for variations of the following:

- A customer rings up with an order for a spare part. (This is a part that, for simplicity, is brought in, re-packaged – the cost of which is to be ignored here – and then sold on.)
- The order quantity is one. The list price is £20 and, with the costing system showing that the part costs £10, a good margin appears to be being made. When the supplier is contacted he is happy to supply at a cost of £10 per unit but has a minimum order quantity of 10. The order is placed for the 10 items at a total cost of £100.
- When the item is sold on to the customer the records show a profit of £10 on the deal.
- But what about the £90 of stock now sitting on the shelf? A year later, when it is still sitting there, the accountant 'writes off' the £90 against current year profit.
- In reality there was no profit on the original order – the business made a loss of £80.

In these types of situation the commercial options need to be considered including:

- Can the price to the customer be increased?
- Can there be a minimum order quantity for our customers?

- Can the minimum order quantity from the supplier be renegotiated?
- Can we afford not to offer these types of products?

Certainly what the business should not be doing is to incentivise the sales team to aggressively sell 'one-offs' of this type – unless it's to get that potentially redundant stock off the shelf!